AWS Certified Cloud Practitioner CLF-C01 Exam Study Guide

Peter Pazurek

Published by Informed Readiness
https://informedreadiness.com
support@informedreadiness.com

© 2023 Informed Readiness

All rights reserved. No portion of this book may be reproduced in any form without permission from the publisher, except as permitted by U.S. copyright law

Dear Reader,

First of all, thank you for choosing my study guide to help you prepare for the AWS Certified Cloud Practitioner CLF-C01 exam. You've made a crucial step towards your certification, and I'm grateful to be part of your journey.

Your success is the reason I have put countless hours into researching, writing, and refining this guide. Every chapter, every paragraph, every sentence has been carefully crafted with your comprehension and retention in mind.

However, my commitment to providing the best learning experience doesn't stop with the last page of this book. I value your feedback to help me improve further.

If you find this guide beneficial, may I ask you to share your experiences with others who may be in a similar situation as you once were? Writing a review on the platform where you purchased this book can make a significant difference to future readers. It gives them insights into the usefulness of this guide and aids their decision-making process.

Thank you once again for your trust, and here's to your successful journey towards becoming an AWS Certified Cloud Practitioner.

Best wishes,
Peter Pazurek

About the Author

Peter Pazurek is a seasoned learning consultant and technical trainer with a diverse background in education and technology. With over 20 years of experience, Peter has dedicated his career to empowering individuals and organizations by helping them harness the power of cutting-edge technologies and build the knowledge and skills they need to work with them.

Based in the vibrant city of Austin, Texas, Peter has worked with a wide range of clients spanning various industries, including startups, Fortune 500 companies, and non-profit organizations.

In addition to his work as a learning consultant, Peter is also a passionate technical trainer. He has designed and delivered numerous training courses, workshops, and seminars for professionals seeking to advance their skills in cloud computing, cybersecurity, enterprise storage, and more.

Peter's passion for technology is matched only by his love for writing. His unique combination of technical expertise and a natural ability to communicate complex ideas in a clear and engaging manner has allowed him to author several books and articles on a variety of technical topics.

When he's not busy consulting and educating, Peter enjoys exploring the beautiful outdoors of Texas, attending live music events in Austin's thriving music scene, and experimenting with the latest gadgets and tech innovations.

Table of Contents

Introduction 5
    About the certification... 5
    About the certification exam.. 5
    Preparing for the certification exam 6
    About the study guide 6
    Exam day tips and strategies 7

Cloud Concepts Exam Domain 10
    Define the AWS Cloud and its value proposition................................... 10
    Identify aspects of AWS Cloud economics.. 21
    Explain the different cloud architecture design principles 31

Technology Exam Domain.. 42
    Define the methods of deploying and operating in the AWS Cloud..... 42
    Define the AWS global infrastructure... 57
    Identify the core AWS services 64
    Identify resources for technology support... 109

Security and Compliance Exam Domain... 120
    Define the AWS shared responsibility model 120
    Define AWS Cloud security and compliance concepts 126
    Identify AWS access management capabilities.................................. 141
    Identify resources for security support.. 151

Billing and Pricing Exam Domain 155
    Compare and contrast the various pricing models for AWS 155
    Recognize the various account structures in relation to AWS billing and pricing 166
    Identify resources available for billing support................................... 171

AWS CLF-C01 Practice Test.. 181
AWS CLF-C01 Practice Test Answer Key 195

Introduction

ATTENTION, this study guide refers to AWS documentation and articles you can access to continue learning about each topic. Go to informedreadiness.com/GetLinks and enter the code **a3b47c** to receive the list of over 300 links to the valuable documents and articles in your email inbox.

This study guide will prepare you to pass the AWS Certified Cloud Practitioner CLF-C01 exam.

About the certification

An AWS Cloud Practitioner is an individual who has foundational knowledge of the AWS Cloud, including the advantages the Cloud offers customers and how customers can design, develop, deploy, and operate solutions in the Cloud. At this point, it's ok if you don't understand what the terms "the cloud," public cloud, and AWS mean. The study guide will define these terms for you in the first exam domain, Cloud Concepts.

The AWS Certified Cloud Practitioner certification is the foundational accreditation from AWS and is applicable to both technical and non-technical staff, IT and business leaders, and anybody who would like to gain a better understanding of the services and resources offered by AWS. Getting the certification is an essential first step to begin working in the AWS Cloud.

About the certification exam

The exam includes a total of 65 questions, including 50 questions that impact your score and 15 unscored questions that do not impact your score. The exam is scored on a scale from 100-1000. The minimum passing score is 700. The number of questions and minimum passing score are subject to change. You can view the current number of questions and passing score in the AWS Certified Cloud Practitioner exam guide at aws.amazon.com/certification/certified-cloud-practitioner.

AWS allows candidates 90 minutes to complete the exam, and the price of the exam is 100 USD. The number of questions and cost are also subject to change. You can view the current duration and price on the AWS Certified Cloud Practitioner web page at aws.amazon.com/certification/certified-cloud-practitioner.

Preparing for the certification exam

Prior to attempting the exam, AWS recommends a candidate should have 6 months experience actively engaging with the AWS Cloud. To gain experience working with AWS, you can create a new account and take advantage of the AWS Free Tier described in the Billing and Pricing exam domain of the study guide. In addition to hands-on experience, AWS recommends reviewing AWS documentation, including user guides, whitepapers, and articles, in order to gain knowledge of the concepts covered on the exam.

About the study guide

The study guide is a direct replacement for the recommendation to review AWS documentation. The guide includes all of the concepts you need to know in order to pass the exam ensuring you don't have to search through multiple documents and sources to find the content you need to study. The study guide contains all of the content you need, including simple explanations of each concept and links to the AWS documentation where the concepts are explained in Amazon's own words.

The study guide follows the same outline as the CLF-C01 exam. In the guide and exam, there are four domains. Within each domain, there are three or four capabilities you must be skilled in to pass the exam. The following list shows how the study guide and exam are outlined.

- Exam Domain: Cloud Concepts
    - ✓ Define the AWS Cloud and its value proposition
    - ✓ Identify aspects of AWS Cloud economics
    - ✓ Explain the different cloud architecture design principles
- Exam Domain: Technology
    - ✓ Define the methods of deploying and operating in the AWS Cloud
    - ✓ Define the AWS global infrastructure
    - ✓ Identify the core AWS services
    - ✓ Identify resources for technology support
- Exam Domain: Security and Compliance
    - ✓ Define the AWS shared responsibility model
    - ✓ Define AWS Cloud security and compliance concepts
    - ✓ Identify AWS access management capabilities
    - ✓ Identify resources for security support
- Exam Domain: Billing and Pricing
    - ✓ Compare and contrast the various pricing models for AWS
    - ✓ Recognize the various account structures in relation to AWS billing and pricing
    - ✓ Identify resources available for billing support

Exam day tips and strategies

Get a good night's sleep
Make sure you get a good night's sleep before the exam to ensure that you are well-rested and alert.

Arrive early
Arrive at the testing center or log in to the remote testing portal early to allow time for any unexpected issues that may arise.

Bring two forms of identification
You will need to present two forms of identification, including one government-issued ID, such as a passport or driver's license.

Take breaks
You will have 90 minutes to complete the exam, and you can take breaks as needed. Use the restroom or grab a drink of water if necessary. Be aware that testing centers may have different rules for leaving the exam room. Review the rules of your chosen test center carefully before using the restroom or leaving the room for a drink of water.

Read each question carefully
Read each question carefully and make sure you understand what is being asked before answering.

Don't spend too much time on one question
The exam consists of 65 questions, so you have approximately 1 minute and 23 seconds to answer each question. If you are stuck on a question, don't spend too much time on it. Mark it for review and move on to the next question. You can always come back to it later.

Answer easy questions first
Start by answering the questions that you find easy and leave the more challenging ones for later. This will help you build up momentum and ensure that you don't get stuck on a single question for too long.

Manage your time
Be aware of the time remaining and make sure you allocate your time accordingly. Don't spend too much time on easy questions and leave yourself enough time for more difficult questions.

Review your answers
Once you have completed the exam, review your answers before submitting. Make sure you have answered every question and check for any mistakes or errors. You will lose points for unanswered questions.

Stay positive

Stay positive and don't let anxiety or stress get the best of you. Take deep breaths and stay focused on the task at hand.

Remember, the key to success on the AWS Certified Cloud Practitioner CLF-C01 exam is preparation and practice. By following these tips and putting in the time and effort to study, you can pass the exam and earn your certification.

Best of luck to you on the exam! And enjoy your time preparing using the AWS Certified Cloud Practitioner CLF-C01 Exam Study Guide.

Cloud Concepts
Exam Domain

Define the AWS Cloud and its value proposition

ATTENTION, this study guide refers to AWS documentation and articles you can access to continue learning about each topic. Go to informedreadiness.com/GetLinks and enter the code **a3b47c** to receive the list of over 300 links to the valuable documents and articles in your email inbox.

Define the cloud

The cloud is a generic term often used to refer to any network that provides wide access to remote technologies, solutions, and services. As it concerns AWS, the cloud is the Internet. The Internet is essentially millions of servers connected together to enable communication and provide customers access to resources, such as websites, email, and social media. AWS uses the Internet to provide customers with access to cloud resources, such as virtual servers or instances to host applications, storage volumes or buckets to store data, and virtual cloud networks to enable communication between cloud resources. As it concerns private cloud services, the cloud is the on-premises infrastructure owned and operated by the organization to provide employees access to cloud resources.

Continue learning about the cloud by browsing the Cloud Definition web page at techterms.com/definition/cloud.

Define cloud computing

As it concerns AWS, cloud computing can be defined as accessing IT resources, such as servers and storage, on-demand over the Internet. IT resources in the cloud, such as virtual servers, are packaged as cloud services. The cloud services are gathered in a service catalog, and the service catalog can be accessed by a user through a web-based portal, such as the AWS Management Console. When a cloud customer wants to provision a cloud resource, they sign in to the portal, select the appropriate service, enter any configuration information required, and launch the resource. In minutes, the cloud resource is made available for the customer to use however and whenever they want. If the customer no longer needs the resource, they can delete it freeing up the underlying infrastructure to be used for future service requests.

Continue learning about the definition of cloud computing by reading the What is Cloud Computing? section of the Overview of Amazon Web Services whitepaper.

Define cloud computing model

A cloud computing model, often referred to as a cloud service model, is essentially a label given to cloud services to define what resources are being offered for customers to use. The cloud computing model defines which components of the cloud architecture the customer is responsible for managing and which components the cloud provider is responsible for managing. The components of the cloud architecture to consider when discussing cloud computing models include servers, storage, networking, virtualization, operating system, middleware, runtime, data, and applications. There are three main cloud computing models used to label cloud services: IaaS, PaaS, and SaaS.

Continue learning about cloud computing models by reading the Types of Cloud Computing section of the Overview of Amazon Web Services whitepaper.

Describe Infrastructure as a Service (IaaS)

IaaS (pronounced eye-az), or Infrastructure as a Service, is a cloud computing model in which the cloud provider is responsible for managing the physical servers, storage, and networking as well as the virtualization technologies used to create multiple resources from the physical infrastructure. The cloud provider offers the use of the infrastructure resources to customers over the Internet as cloud services. A customer can utilize the cloud services for their infrastructure-based cloud computing use case, such as launching virtual server instances to host applications and creating buckets or storage volumes to store data. Common AWS IaaS services include Amazon EC2 for computing, Amazon S3 for storage, and Amazon VPC for networking.

Continue learning about Infrastructure as a Service by browsing the Cloud Computing Models section of the Types of Cloud Computing web page at aws.amazon.com/types-of-cloud-computing/.

Describe Platform as a Service (PaaS)

PaaS (pronounced paz), or Platform as a Service, is a cloud computing model in which the cloud provider is responsible for managing the physical server, storage, and networking, as well as the virtualization technologies, operating system, middleware, and runtime resources. The cloud provider offers the use of the operating system, middleware, and runtime resources to customers over the Internet as cloud services. A customer can utilize the services for their platform-based cloud computing use case, such as developing, testing, and running applications. Common AWS PaaS services include Amazon ECS and Amazon EKS for containerized applications and AWS Lambda for serverless code execution.

Continue learning about Platform as a Service by browsing the Cloud Computing Models section of the Types of Cloud Computing web page at aws.amazon.com/types-of-cloud-computing/.

Describe Software as a Service (SaaS)

SaaS (pronounced sass), or Software as a Service, is a cloud computing model in which the cloud provider is responsible for managing the entire cloud computing architecture, including physical networking, server, and storage devices, the virtualization tools, operating system, middleware, runtime, data, and application resources. The cloud provider offers the use of the application resources to customers over the Internet as cloud services. A customer can utilize the services for their software-based cloud computing use case, such as backing up data, emailing contacts, and detecting malware on a device. Common AWS SaaS services include Amazon Connect to provide customer service with a cloud contact center and AWS Service Catalog to provide users access to an approved catalog of IT services, applications, and resources deployed in the AWS Cloud.

Continue learning about Software as a Service by browsing the Software-as-a-Service (SaaS) on AWS web page at aws.amazon.com/solutions/saas/.

Define cloud computing deployment model

A cloud computing deployment model is a label given to cloud platforms, like AWS, to define where the infrastructure hosting the cloud platform is located. The cloud deployment model also defines who owns and operates the infrastructure and who can access the cloud services hosted on the platform. There are three cloud deployment models recognized by AWS: Cloud, On-premises, and Hybrid.

Continue learning about cloud computing deployment models by browsing the Cloud Computing Deployment Models section of the Types of Cloud Computing web page at aws.amazon.com/types-of-cloud-computing/.

Describe the Cloud deployment model

What AWS refers to as the cloud deployment model is often referred to as public cloud. With the cloud deployment model, the infrastructure is located in one or more data centers owned and operated by the public cloud provider, like AWS. The cloud services are offered to any customer in the general public that has access to the Internet. This deployment model is ideal for single users who would like to take advantage of the benefits of cloud computing, organizations without the budget, time, or knowledge to support IT infrastructure, or anybody that would like to take advantage of the wide global access provided by the cloud deployment model.

Continue learning about cloud computing deployment models by browsing the Cloud Computing Deployment Models section of the Types of Cloud Computing webpage at aws.amazon.com/types-of-cloud-computing/.

Describe the On-premises deployment model

What AWS refers to as the on-premises deployment model is often referred to as private cloud. With the on-premises deployment model, the infrastructure is located in one or more data centers owned or leased by a single organization. All components in the infrastructure are owned or leased by the organization and are operated by employees or contractors. The cloud services are only offered to employees and contractors of the organization. This deployment model is more expensive than public cloud and requires a great deal more time and effort for acquisition and operation. On-premises deployment is ideal for organizations who require complete control over their infrastructure and data, must meet compliance requirements not met by a public cloud provider, and have the expertise and budget to own and operate on-premises cloud infrastructure.

Continue learning about cloud computing deployment models by browsing the Cloud Computing Deployment Models section of the Types of Cloud Computing webpage at aws.amazon.com/types-of-cloud-computing/.

Describe the Hybrid deployment model

The hybrid deployment model is a combination of the other two models, cloud and on-premises. With the hybrid deployment model, organizations integrate their private on-premises cloud platform with a public cloud platform using migration tools to move applications, data, and other workloads between the cloud platforms. This deployment model is ideal for organizations who would like to take advantage of the benefits of public cloud but have critical applications and sensitive data that require the use of on-premises infrastructure. A common use case for hybrid cloud is an organization integrating AWS with their private cloud to quickly scale, or grow, their IT infrastructure to handle increased activity. For example, a retail company may adopt hybrid cloud and deploy web servers in the AWS Cloud around the holidays to handle the temporary increase in activity generated from online shopping. AWS offers several hybrid cloud services to simplify migrating resources, applications, and data between customers' on-premises environment and the AWS Cloud, such as AWS DataSync to simplify and accelerate secure data migrations and VMware Cloud on AWS to rapidly migrate virtual machines between the two environments.

Continue learning about the AWS hybrid cloud services by browsing the AWS Hybrid Cloud web page at aws.amazon.com/hybrid/.

Define elasticity

Elasticity is a characteristic of every cloud computing model which means cloud resources can grow or shrink to quickly adapt to demand with little to no human interaction. As an operator of cloud infrastructure, this means workflows should be automated and the technologies in the infrastructure should work in orchestration to make IT resources quickly available to the customer of the cloud services. As a cloud customer, this means when more resources are needed, like storage or compute, they can be added to the existing infrastructure quickly and easily. Elasticity does not only refer to growing resources. It also refers to shrinking resources. When a customer no longer needs a resource, the resource should automatically be added back to the pool of resources in the cloud infrastructure to be made available for other cloud customers. Some AWS resources automatically grow and shrink as part of the service to adapt to demand, such as Amazon S3 and Amazon Aurora storage. Other AWS services don't grow or shrink automatically by default but can be grown quickly by making minor changes to the configuration of the resource, such as Amazon EC2 and Amazon RDS instances. AWS Auto Scaling is a service that helps achieve elasticity by enabling customers to automatically grow and shrink capacity for supported AWS services, such as Amazon EC2 and Amazon DynamoDB.

Continue learning about elasticity by browsing the What is Cloud Elasticity? web page at vmware.com/topics/glossary/content/cloud-elasticity/.

Define high availability

Availability refers to a technology being ready to use for its intended purpose. High availability refers to ensuring technologies experience as little down time as possible in providing service to an organization. Cloud infrastructure achieves high availability by clustering several components into a pool of resources to ensure cloud services can be restored quickly if a failure or service disruption should occur. AWS customers can achieve high availability when operating in the cloud by launching redundant resources in multiple Availability Zones. Some AWS services achieve high availability as part of the service by automatically storing copies of resources in multiple Availability Zones, such as Amazon S3, Amazon EBS, and Amazon DynamoDB. AWS customers can achieve high availability when developing in the AWS cloud by decoupling applications and developing distributed systems using services like Amazon SQS, Amazon SNS, and Amazon API Gateway.

Continue learning about high availability by browsing the High Availability in the Cloud web page at scandio.de/blog/en/2021/07/high-availability.

Define fault tolerance

Fault tolerance is a measure of availability. Unlike high availability, which allows for a certain amount of downtime, fault tolerance refers to experiencing no service disruption if a component fails. Cloud infrastructure achieves fault tolerance by having redundant resources and mechanisms to automatically fail over to a backup resource if there is a fault with the primary. For example, cloud infrastructure will typically have multiple servers physically connected together and configured the same with access to the same resources. A mechanism will monitor the primary server that is providing services to the cloud customers. When the mechanism detects a failure, it will initiate a failover to the backup, all workflows will be moved to the backup, the backup becomes the primary component, and begins providing services to the cloud customers. AWS customers can deploy fault tolerant compute systems by launching redundant compute resources in multiple Availability Zones or by using Auto Scaling to automatically launch additional compute resources if any should fail. They can also achieve fault tolerance by using Elastic Load Balancers to detect when a compute resource is not healthy and spread traffic across only healthy resources.

Continue learning about fault tolerance by browsing the What is Fault Tolerance? web page at avinetworks.com/glossary/fault-tolerance/.

Define scalability

Scalability refers to the ability to grow or shrink IT infrastructure as demand changes and resources require more or less capacity. Cloud computing provides high scalability potential to customers due to the elastic and on-demand characteristics of cloud resources. A cloud customer can quickly scale out their infrastructure from the seat of their chair by adding additional resources, like a new virtual server, without disrupting service or going through a long procurement process. A customer can also quickly scale up by increasing the capacity of their existing resources, such as provisioned storage volume space or memory assigned to a virtual server. At first glance, elasticity and scalability seem like two terms with the same meaning, and they are similar. The main difference is scalability refers to the ability to grow or shrink to meet demand by manually adding additional resources in a pre-planned manner. Elasticity refers to the ability to grow or shrink resources dynamically by automatically adding or removing capacity to adapt to changing demand.

Continue learning about scalability by browsing the What is Cloud Scalability? web page at vmware.com/topics/glossary/content/cloud-scalability/.

Define agility

In cloud computing, agility refers to the ability to quickly adapt to changes and to rapidly deploy resources to drive business growth while developing and operating in the cloud. With traditional IT infrastructure, organizations often have to wait weeks or even months for hardware to arrive on site before new applications and services can be deployed. With AWS, customers can quickly scale their resources up as demand increases and scale down when demand decreases. This ensures new infrastructure, applications, and services can be deployed with great agility. The agility AWS enables also ensures customers can quickly, easily, and cost-effectively deploy the resources they need for testing, staging, and production environments. This level of agility is nearly impossible to achieve at the same cost with traditional IT infrastructure.

Continue learning about agility by reading the Business Agility section of the Business Value on AWS eBook.

Define AWS

AWS, or Amazon Web Services, is a public cloud platform providing IT resources over the Internet to individuals and organizations across the globe. The AWS Cloud is secure, elastic, highly available, fault tolerant, and empowers customers to efficiently scale their infrastructure and applications to fit their evolving needs. AWS offers services that enable customers to build highly available, fault tolerant solutions with great agility to optimize staff productivity and operational resilience. AWS began offering cloud computing services to businesses in 2006. In 2022, AWS offers over 200 fully featured services and serves customers in 245 countries and territories across the globe.

Continue learning about AWS by browsing the What is AWS web page at aws.amazon.com/what-is-aws/.

List the categories of AWS Foundation Services

The AWS Foundation Services fall into the following four categories, compute, storage, databases, and networking.

Continue learning about the categories of services offered by AWS by browsing the Cloud Products web page at aws.amazon.com/products/. Use the checkbox filters under Technology Categories to view which services are in each category.

Describe compute in relation to AWS

As it concerns IT infrastructure, compute typically refers to servers and other components that provide services to devices in the organization by hosting applications, processing data, and fulfilling requests for a wide variety of IT services. AWS offers several compute services to achieve the same goal in the cloud and to provide a platform for developers to develop, deploy, run, and scale applications with great agility. Common AWS foundational compute services include Amazon EC2 for hosting virtual server instances, Amazon ECS for managing and orchestrating containers, and AWS Lambda for code execution with serverless computing.

Continue learning about compute in relation to AWS by browsing the What is Compute? web page at aws.amazon.com/what-is/compute/.

Describe storage in relation to AWS

Storage in regards to IT infrastructure refers to a centralized repository for data stored and accessed by devices throughout an organization. Data is most often stored, organized, and presented in one of three formats: block, file, or object. Common AWS foundational storage services include Amazon S3 to make high-capacity object storage available to users and applications across the Internet at a low cost, Amazon EBS to provide high performing block storage for applications and services running on EC2 instances, and Amazon EFS to provide a file system and file storage to applications and users who require access to large content repositories and home directories.

Continue learning about storage in relation to AWS by browsing the What is Cloud Storage? web page at aws.amazon.com/what-is-cloud-storage/.

Describe databases in relation to AWS

A database is a collection of data organized in a structured manner. Applications use databases to store many types of data and rely on the structure of the database to quickly and easily record, find, and change data stored in the database. AWS offers database services with a focus on performance, availability, reliability, and security to suit the needs of any type of application developed, tested, or deployed in the cloud or on-premises. Common AWS foundational database services include Amazon RDS to provide scalable relational databases for traditional applications, Amazon Redshift to provide relational databases for data warehousing, and Amazon DynamoDB to provide key-value databases for high traffic applications.

Continue learning about databases in relation to AWS by browsing the Purpose-Built Databases on AWS web page at aws.amazon.com/products/databases/.

Describe networking in relation to AWS

Networking refers to facilitating the transfer of data between devices. In terms of IT infrastructure, networking most often consists of switches and routers facilitating data transfer between computers, servers, and storage devices in the organization. AWS offers networking services with a focus on securing data transfer between cloud services, ensuring availability of data and content throughout the cloud, and optimizing performance of data transfer and content delivery. Common AWS foundational networking services include Amazon VPC to provide a secure virtual network for AWS resources to communicate with each other, Amazon CloudFront to deliver high performing content to applications and users across the globe, and AWS Direct Connect to provide a dedicated network connection between customers' on-premises environment and the AWS Cloud.

Continue learning about networking in relations to AWS by browsing the What is Computer Networking? web page at aws.amazon.com/what-is/computer-networking/.

Identify aspects of AWS Cloud economics

List the six advantages of cloud computing recognized by AWS

The six advantages of cloud computing recognized by AWS include stop guessing capacity, increase speed and agility, go global in minutes, trade fixed expense for variable expense, benefit from massive economies of scale, and stop spending money running and maintaining data centers.

Continue learning about the six advantages of cloud computing with AWS by reading the Six Advantages of Cloud Computing section of the Overview of Amazon Web Services whitepaper.

Describe the AWS advantage stop guessing capacity

When planning for infrastructure and applications in traditional IT, organizations need to make a decision up front on how much capacity they think they need. Organizations need to determine how many servers and how much memory and processing capacity they need, how many switches and how much throughput capacity they need, and how many storage devices and how much storage capacity they need. With this approach, organizations can run into issues on both ends of the spectrum. They can waste time and money on extra capacity they don't need, or they can approach the limits of available capacity and need to reduce the functionality of their environment while they procure more resources. With AWS, certain services require no capacity planning and resources grow and shrink automatically as the resource is utilized, like Amazon S3 buckets and Amazon RDS DB instances. With other AWS services, customers still make a decision about how much capacity they need when they launch a resource, like Amazon EC2 instances. However, the customer can quickly add or remove capacity manually or automatically using services like AWS Auto Scaling which automatically adjusts compute capacity based on the needs of the infrastructure and applications. With all AWS services, the scalability of the AWS Cloud ensures customers avoid paying for resources they don't use or slowing production due to reaching capacity limits.

Continue learning about how AWS ensures customers can stop guessing capacity and how easy it is to add capacity to AWS resources by reading the Change the instance type section of the Amazon Elastic Compute Cloud User Guide for Windows Instances.

Describe the AWS advantage increase speed and agility

Planning and procuring traditional IT resources can take weeks. Installing, testing, and deploying the resources takes additional time before they become available for use by developers and other users in the organization. With AWS, customers can deploy IT resources in the cloud from the seat of their chair making them available for development, test, or production environments in minutes. AWS also offers services that increase the speed and agility that cloud administrators can deploy systems and developers can build and launch applications. AWS Lambda, for example, is a serverless compute service that allows customers to run code without provisioning or managing servers enabling them to focus more time on developing applications that help the business and less time on managing infrastructure.

Continue learning about how AWS increases speed and agility and how quickly you can launch an AWS resource by reading Working with buckets, Creating a bucket section of the Amazon Simple Storage Service User Guide.

Describe the AWS advantage go global in minutes

In IT there is a concept called attenuation which ultimately results in lower performance the further users are away from a resource, like a server or storage device. If an organization has a data center in the United States and has users in Singapore, they would also need a data center in Singapore to provide the same user experience as they provide their users in the U.S. AWS has data centers in multiple Regions all over the world. When a customer provisions a resource in the AWS Cloud, they launch the resource in the Region they want the resource to reside in. If an AWS customer in the United States has users in Singapore, they can quickly and easily provision an AWS resource in Singapore to provide the same user experience to those users as they provide to the users in the U.S. Many AWS services also have features that enable customers to quickly make a resource available in another Region, such as replication and Multi-Region Access Points. If a customer can't deploy resources in each Region where they have users, they can use services like Amazon CloudFront which is a content delivery network (CDN) enabling them to deliver their content with low latency and high transfer speeds across the world.

Continue learning about how AWS enables customers to go global in minutes by reading Regions in the Networking, Regions and Zones section of the Amazon Elastic Compute Cloud User Guide for Windows Instances.

Describe the AWS advantage trade fixed expense for variable expense

In traditional IT, a lot of time and money goes into planning and procuring IT infrastructure, like data centers and servers, with high upfront cost classified as fixed, or capital, expense. With capital expense, IT organizations run the risk of spending more for services they may never use. With the AWS pay-as-you-go pricing model, customers have no upfront costs. Instead, customers trade capital expense for variable expenses and only pay for the infrastructure and services they use while they are using them. For example, with Amazon EC2 customers can quickly and easily scale their computing capacity up or down based on demand, and only pay for the capacity they use. Paying monthly for the AWS resources they use ensures customers don't waste valuable time and money on IT infrastructure unless it is of immediate benefit to their users and applications. Paying monthly also ensures customers have fewer long-term cost obligations and can focus funds on new investments and innovation.

Continue learning about how AWS enables customers to trade capital expense for variable expense by reading the AWS blog New - Per Second Billing for EC2 Instances and EBS Volumes.

Describe the AWS advantage benefit from massive economies of scale

With most commerce, the price per unit of an asset gets lower as a customer buys more of the asset. The same notion applies to purchasing IT infrastructure. If an organization purchases 100 servers at a time, the price of each server will be lower resulting in a lower total cost than if the organization purchased one server at a time to eventually procure 100 servers. Due to serving a massive number of cloud customers across the globe, AWS is able to purchase IT infrastructure in large quantities much greater than most traditional IT organizations can acquire. In purchasing large quantities and lowering their own expense, AWS passes the savings on to the customer with lower pricing options for the cloud resources they consume.

Continue learning about how AWS customers benefit from massive economies of scale by reading the AWS blog Amazon EC2 – 15 Years of Optimizing and Saving Your IT Costs.

Describe the AWS advantage stop spending money running and maintaining data centers

In traditional IT, cost goes well beyond purchasing technologies. An organization has to purchase or lease the use of a data center to host the technologies and pay for heating, ventilation, cooling systems, electricity, and other utilities. They have to pay the salary and benefits for people to work in the data center installing and maintaining the technologies. They also have to pay to replace the technologies as they reach the end of their lifecycle. AWS assumes the burden of running and maintaining data centers across the world on behalf of all AWS customers. This empowers customers to focus on operating their business without worrying about operating infrastructure.

Continue learning about how AWS helps customers stop spending money on running and maintaining data centers by browsing the How Much Does Running A Private Data Center Cost Per Year web page at streamdatacenters.com/glossary/data-center-cost/.

Describe the benefits of AWS pay-as-you-go pricing

With AWS pay-as-you-go pricing, often referred to as on-demand pricing, a customer only pays for the resources they use while they are using them. For example, a customer can launch an EC2 instance and only pay for compute time while the instance is up and running. AWS pay-as-you-go pricing ensures a customer will not pay for resources they do not use and ensures there is no long-term commitment, minimum fee, or upfront cost. Pay-as-you-go pricing reduces the risk of overprovisioning resources and enables resources and expenditures to grow along with a growing business.

Continue learning about AWS pay-as-you-go pricing by browsing the Pay-as-you-go section of the AWS Pricing web page at aws.amazon.com/pricing/.

Describe AWS tiered pricing

AWS uses tiered pricing to determine billing for many of the services they offer. The tiered pricing provides volume discounts for customers based on criteria such as the amount of the resource consumed, how often the resource is accessed, and the duration the resource has been in service. For example, AWS bills for S3 standard storage at a progressively lower rate based on the amount of data stored. The first 50 TB stored in an S3 bucket in a month are billed at a certain price per GB. The price of the next 450 TB stored in the same month is lower per GB, and any storage over 500 TB is even lower still.

Continue learning about the AWS tiered pricing by browsing the Pay less by using more section of the AWS Pricing web page at aws.amazon.com/pricing/.

Compare capital expenditures (CapEx) with operating expenses (OpEx)

Capital expenditures, or CapEx, are an organization's long-term purchases, such as servers, storage, and networking devices, and any maintenance costs that extend the life of the asset, such as upgraded components and additional licensing. Operating expenses, or OpEx, are the ongoing costs of operating the asset, like monitoring health status or provisioning resources. With CapEx, an organization pays significant upfront cost for assets forcing them to commit to a solution and leaving little cash for new investments and innovation. By focusing more funding on OpEx, an organization can make smaller investments over time with no upfront cost or obligation allowing for the organization to be more agile and make changes and improvements in evolving markets, like Information Technology.

Continue learning about CapEx and OpEx by browsing the CapEx vs. OpEx - Key Considerations for Your Cloud Cost Management web page at cloudhealthtech.com/blog/capex-vs-opex-cloud-cost-management/.

Define Total Cost of Ownership (TCO)

Total Cost of Ownership, or TCO, is a calculation that shows the cost of an asset over time by adding the purchase price of the asset and the cost of maintaining it, known as capital expenditures, with the cost of operating the asset, known as operating expenses. TCO is often used to analyze and compare the cost of two similar assets or solutions to determine which one is the most cost effective, and ultimately to make a business decision regarding which one to purchase. TCO analysis is a methodology often used to compare the cost of developing and operating in the AWS Cloud to the cost of acquiring, operating, and maintaining on-premises infrastructure to show the cost savings customers experience when choosing AWS over on-premises infrastructure.

Continue learning about Total Cost of Ownership by browsing the Total Cost of Ownership (TCO) web page at investopedia.com/terms/t/totalcostofownership.

Identify the costs included in TCO of traditional IT

TCO of traditional IT goes beyond the cost of purchasing components, such as servers, storage, and networking devices. An organization not only owns the infrastructure, they also operate and maintain the components and any installed software. This equates to additional cost adding to the total in the form of labor hours to deploy, administer, and maintain the infrastructure. Also adding to the total cost is licensing any software installed, such as virtualization, operating system, and application software. With on-premises infrastructure, an organization also must factor in the cost of overhead, such as power, cooling, and buying or leasing data center space.

Continue learning about TCO of IT by browsing the Total Cost of Ownership (TCO)? SUSE Defines web page at suse.com/suse-defines/definition/total-cost-ownership-tco/.

Describe how AWS customers optimize TCO of IT by rightsizing infrastructure

AWS customers optimize TCO of Information Technology in many ways, such as rightsizing infrastructure. The elasticity of AWS services enables customers to grow and shrink their infrastructure resources as demand changes. Customers can manually increase or decrease the capacity of their infrastructure resources to meet demand as they monitor their environment using their own tools or AWS tools and features, such as Cost Explorer rightsizing recommendations for EC2 instances. Rightsizing recommendations for EC2 instances enables customers to match workloads to the appropriate EC2 instance type to achieve the best balance of cost and performance. Customers can also use AWS services and features, like Auto Scaling, to automatically right size their infrastructure to meet changing demand. By automatically scaling resources, AWS customers ensure their infrastructure is always the right size in order to only pay for the exact capacity they need to service their users and applications.

Continue learning about rightsizing AWS infrastructure by browsing the Right Sizing web page at aws.amazon.com/aws-cost-management/aws-cost-optimization/right-sizing/.

Describe how automation in the AWS Cloud optimizes TCO of IT

Automation refers to reducing human intervention in processes and procedures. In IT, automation is used to perform repeatable tasks consistently and successfully. Automating repeatable tasks optimizes TCO of IT by reducing human error that can result in extra time and money to fix issues and by freeing up staff to innovate and complete tasks that require human intervention and can't be automated. Automation often ensures customers don't need to hire additional IT staff to operate and troubleshoot solutions resulting in lower labor costs. AWS offers several services and features to automate common tasks while operating and developing in the Cloud. AWS CloudFormation, for example, enables customers to automate the deployment of infrastructure resources to build AWS IT environments in a repeatable fashion. AWS CodeDeploy enables customers to deploy software across environments ensuring applications and services are released with minimal errors and issues. AWS customers can automate compliance and security tasks with several services and features, such as AWS Config, AWS Inspector, and AWS CloudTrail.

Continue learning about how automation in the AWS Cloud optimizes TCO of IT by reading the AWS blog The Case for Investing in Cloud Automation.

Describe how reducing AWS customers' compliance responsibility optimizes TCO of IT

Compliance refers to the responsibility an organization has to remain in accordance with certain guidelines and specifications. Compliance guidelines and specifications vary by industry and location and are established and regulated by a standards body, like a nation's government. Organizations must remain in compliance with the regulations imposed upon them by the industries they operate in and by the countries where they do business. In IT, compliance regulations include guidelines and specifications that must be met for the data center, hardware, software, data, and people that work with the technologies and facilities. Remaining in compliance costs money in terms of monitoring, reporting, auditing, and other security controls that must be in place to ensure all components of the IT environment are in compliance with the regulations imposed upon the organization. AWS provides a shared responsibility model for security and compliance. AWS customers are responsible for the compliance and compliance costs of their environments, applications, services, and data they deploy and operate in the AWS Cloud. However, AWS assumes the compliance responsibility of the data center and infrastructure that hosts the AWS Cloud. By assuming the compliance responsibility of the AWS Cloud infrastructure and the data centers where it resides, AWS reduces both the customer's compliance responsibility and their cost of remaining in compliance.

Continue learning about how AWS reduces customers' compliance responsibility and optimizes TCO of IT by reading the Compliance section of the Introduction to AWS Security whitepaper.

Describe how AWS helps customers save on software licensing costs

Enterprise software, such as Microsoft Windows Server operating systems and Microsoft SQL Server database management systems, require customers to purchase licenses to unlock the features and functionality of the software. The licenses come with a high upfront cost and often require periodic, ongoing renewal fees to continue using the software or to add new features and apply upgrades. AWS has documented case studies in which customers have reduced licensing cost for enterprise software by 40% or more saving millions of dollars annually by using the AWS Cloud. AWS helps customers save on software licensing costs by eliminating large investments in upfront licensing costs for Amazon EC2 instances running Microsoft Windows Server and Amazon RDS database instances running Microsoft SQL Server. With EC2, customers can launch license included instances running Windows Server with the license already installed and included in the monthly price of the instance. With RDS, customers can also launch license included instances running SQL Server with the license already installed and included in the monthly price. License included instances ensure the customer has no upfront cost or long-term investment on software licensing.

Continue learning about how AWS helps customers save on software licensing costs by browsing the Microsoft Licensing on AWS web page at aws.amazon.com/windows/resources/licensing/.

Describe how AWS fully managed services help reduce TCO

Enterprise applications and services require a platform to run on. Microsoft SQL Server, for example, is installed and runs on an operating system, such as Microsoft

Windows Server. The operating system as well as the enterprise application must be updated and patched by somebody to ensure the features are up to date and any security vulnerabilities have been remediated. If an issue arises with the operating system or the application, somebody has to troubleshoot the issue and resolve it to ensure it doesn't happen again. To complete all of these management tasks, organizations must keep skilled operations personnel on staff increasing the total cost of ownership of the enterprise application. With AWS fully managed services, AWS performs all management tasks for the application or service and the platform it runs on. When a customer launches a resource with a fully managed service, the resource is automatically provisioned with the application already installed. After the resource is launched, AWS is responsible for upgrading, patching, and troubleshooting the application or service and the platform it runs on. By removing the burden of managing these tasks, AWS customers reduce the cost of operations and can spend more time and money on innovation and growing the business. AWS offers many fully managed services to help customers save on operating costs, including Amazon RDS for relational databases, Amazon DynamoDB for NoSQL databases, Amazon ECS for Docker containers, and Amazon EKS for Kubernetes container orchestration.

Continue learning about how AWS fully managed services help reduce TCO by reading the Graze Case Study at aws.amazon.com/solutions/case-studies/graze/.

Explain the different cloud architecture design principles

Define the AWS Well-Architected Framework

The AWS Well-Architected Framework is a set of design principles and best practices AWS recommends following when designing and operating solutions in the AWS Cloud. The framework consists of six pillars that are imperative to follow in order to build stable and efficient solutions. The six pillars are Operational Excellence, Security, Reliability, Performance Efficiency, Cost Optimization, and Sustainability. By following the six pillars, AWS customers can make informed decisions and design solutions that meet their expectations and requirements.

Continue learning about what the AWS Well-Architected Framework is by browsing the AWS Well-Architected web page at aws.amazon.com/architecture/well-architected/.

Define workload

The term workload is used throughout the AWS Well-Architected Framework and in other AWS documentation and content. In cloud computing, the term workload refers to all components and resources of a solution that work together to provide business value. In the AWS Cloud, a workload is typically one or more resources provisioned with AWS services working together as one solution, such as multiple EC2 instances each running a different component of an application with an S3 bucket storing application data.

Continue learning about what a workload is by reading the definitions of common AWS architecture terms in the Abstraction and Introduction, Definitions section of the AWS Well-Architect Framework whitepaper.

List the general design principles in the AWS Well-Architected Framework

There are six general design principles in the AWS Well-Architected Framework: stop guessing your capacity needs, test systems at production scale, automate to make architectural experimentation easier, allow for evolutionary architectures, drive architectures using data, and improve through game days.

Continue learning about the general design principles by reading the Abstract and Introduction, General design principles section of the AWS Well-Architected Framework whitepaper.

Define the Operational Excellence pillar of the AWS Well-Architected Framework

IT Operations refers to a function in an organization in which teams of individuals ensure IT services are delivered effectively and efficiently. Operations teams are responsible for varying levels of administering, maintaining, monitoring, and troubleshooting issues with the infrastructure and services supporting the organization. The AWS Operational Excellence pillar includes design principles and best practice areas to ensure AWS customers continually improve processes and procedures for operating their provisioned AWS environment to deliver business value to their customers.

Continue learning about what the Operational Excellence pillar is by reading The Pillars of the Framework, Operational Excellence, Definition section of the AWS Well-Architected Framework whitepaper.

List the design principles in the Operational Excellence pillar

The Operational Excellence pillar of the AWS Well-Architected Framework includes five design principles for operational excellence in the cloud: perform operations as code, make frequent, small, reversible changes, refine operations procedures frequently, anticipate failure, and learn from all operational failures.

Continue learning about the design principles in the Operational Excellence pillar by reading about each principle in The Pillars of the Framework, Operational Excellence, Design Principles section of the AWS Well-Architected Framework whitepaper.

List the best practice areas in the Operational Excellence pillar

The Operational Excellence pillar of the AWS Well-Architected Framework includes four best practice areas for operational excellence in the cloud: Organization, Prepare, Operate, and Evolve.

Continue learning about the best practice areas in the Operational Excellence pillar by reading about each practice in The Pillars of the Framework, Operational Excellence, Best Practices section of the AWS Well-Architected Framework whitepaper.

Define the Security pillar of the AWS Well-Architected Framework

Security refers to protecting the confidentiality, integrity, and availability of information, systems, and assets. The AWS Security pillar includes design principles and best practice areas to assess and mitigate the risk of security events impacting AWS systems, data, and other assets.

Continue learning about what the Security pillar is by reading The Pillars of the Framework, Security, Definition section of the AWS Well-Architected Framework whitepaper.

List the design principles in the Security pillar

The Security pillar of the AWS Well-Architected Framework includes seven design principles for security in the cloud: implement a strong identity foundation, enable traceability, apply security at all layers, automate security best practices, protect data in transit and at rest, keep people away from data, and prepare for security events.

Continue learning about the design principles in the Security pillar by reading about each principle in The Pillars of the Framework, Security, Design Principles section of the AWS Well-Architected Framework whitepaper.

List the best practice areas in the Security pillar

The Security pillar of the AWS Well-Architected Framework includes six best practice areas for security in the cloud: Security, Identity and Access Management, Detective Controls, Infrastructure Protection, Data Protection, and Incident Response.

Continue learning about the best practice areas in the Security pillar by reading about each practice in The Pillars of the Framework, Security, Best Practices section of the AWS Well-Architected Framework whitepaper.

Define the Reliability pillar of the AWS Well-Architected Framework

Reliability refers to AWS customers' ability to consistently deliver service to their users or customers. The AWS Reliability pillar includes design principles and best practice areas to ensure customers can quickly recover from a failure or service disruption and prevent complete outages of service delivery.

Continue learning about what the Reliability pillar is by reading the Reliability, Definitions section as well as the three topics within the section in the Reliability Pillar - AWS Well-Architected Framework whitepaper.

List the design principles in the Reliability pillar

The Reliability pillar of the AWS Well-Architected Framework includes five design principles for reliability in the cloud: automatically recover from a failure, test recovery procedures, scale horizontally to increase aggregate workload availability, stop guessing capacity, and manage change in automation.

Continue learning about the design principles in the Reliability pillar by reading about each principle in The Pillars of the Framework, Reliability, Design Principles section of the AWS Well-Architected Framework whitepaper.

List the best practice areas in the Reliability pillar

The Reliability pillar of the AWS Well-Architected Framework includes four best practice areas for reliability in the cloud: Foundations, Workload Architecture, Change Management, and Failure Management.

Continue learning about the best practice areas in the Reliability pillar by reading about each practice in The Pillars of the Framework, Reliability, Best Practices section of the AWS Well-Architected Framework whitepaper.

Define the Performance Efficiency pillar of the AWS Well-Architected Framework

Performance refers to the ability to meet demand and process requests in the expected amount of time. The AWS Performance Efficiency pillar includes design principles and best practice areas to ensure AWS customers always have the compute resources they need to sustain performance when demand increases and environments change.

Continue learning about what the Performance Efficiency pillar is by reading The Pillars of the Framework, Performance Efficiency, Definition section of the AWS Well-Architected Framework whitepaper.

List the design principles in the Performance Efficiency pillar

The Performance Efficiency pillar of the AWS Well-Architected Framework includes five design principles for performance efficiency in the cloud: democratize advanced technologies, go global in minutes, use serverless architectures, experiment more often, and mechanical sympathy.

Continue learning about the design principles in the Performance Efficiency pillar by reading about each principle in The Pillars of the Framework, Performance Efficiency, Design Principles section of the AWS Well-Architected Framework whitepaper.

List the best practice areas in the Performance Efficiency pillar

The Performance Efficiency pillar of the AWS Well-Architected Framework includes four best practice areas for performance efficiency in the cloud: Selection, Review, Monitoring, and Tradeoffs.

Continue learning about the best practice areas in the Performance Efficiency pillar by reading The Pillars of the Framework, Performance Efficiency, Best Practices section of the AWS Well-Architected Framework whitepaper.

Define the Cost Optimization pillar of the AWS Well-Architected Framework

Cost refers to the price AWS customers pay for the resources they use to deliver their business. The AWS Cost Optimization pillar includes design principles and best practice areas to ensure customers optimize cost in the AWS Cloud and pay the lowest price possible for the cloud resources they consume.

Continue learning about what the Cost Optimization pillar is by reading The Pillars of the Framework, Cost Optimization, Definition section of the AWS Well-Architected Framework whitepaper.

List the design principles in the Cost Optimization pillar

The Cost Optimization pillar of the AWS Well-Architected Framework includes five design principles for cost optimization in the cloud: implement cloud financial management, adopt a consumption model, measure overall efficiency, stop spending money on undifferentiated heavy lifting, and analyze and attribute expenditure.

Continue learning about the design principles in the Cost Optimization pillar by reading about each principle in The Pillars of the Framework, Cost Optimization, Design Principles section of the AWS Well-Architected Framework whitepaper.

List the best practice areas in the Cost Optimization pillar

The Cost Optimization pillar of the AWS Well-Architected Framework includes five best practice areas for cost optimization in the cloud: Practice Cloud Financial Management, Expenditure and Usage Awareness, Cost-Effective Resources, Manage Demand and Supply Resources, and Optimize Over Time.

Continue learning about the best practice areas in the Cost Optimization pillar by reading about each practice in The Pillars of the Framework, Cost Optimization, Best Practices section of the AWS Well-Architected Framework whitepaper.

Define the Sustainability pillar of the AWS Well-Architected Framework

Sustainability refers to meeting the needs of the present without negatively impacting the future in terms of environmental, economic, and social impact. The Sustainability pillar of the AWS Well-Architected framework includes design principles and best practice areas to ensure customers design and operate solutions in the AWS Cloud that will achieve maximum benefit while provisioning as few resources as possible to meet expectations and requirements. The primary sustainability objective in the Sustainability pillar is energy reduction and efficiency across all components of a solution.

Continue learning about what the Sustainability pillar is by reading the Cloud sustainability section of the Sustainability Pillar - AWS Well-Architected Framework whitepaper.

List the design principles in the Sustainability pillar

The Sustainability pillar of the AWS Well-Architected Framework includes six design principles for sustainability in the cloud: understand your impact, establish sustainable goals, maximize utilization, anticipate and adopt new, more efficient hardware and software offerings, use managed services, and reduce the downstream impact of your cloud workloads.

Continue learning about the design principles in the Sustainability pillar by reading about each principle in The Pillars of the Framework, Sustainability, Design Principles section of the AWS Well-Architected Framework whitepaper.

List the best practice areas in the Sustainability pillar

The Performance Efficiency pillar of the AWS Well-Architected Framework includes seven best practice areas for performance efficiency in the cloud: Region Selection, User Behavior Patterns, Software and Architecture Patterns, Data Patterns, Hardware Patterns, Development and deployment patterns, and Resources.

Continue learning about the best practice areas in the Sustainability pillar by reading about each practice in The Pillars of the Framework, Sustainability, Best Practices section of the AWS Well-Architected Framework whitepaper.

Describe how customers can design for failure in the AWS Cloud

A failure in IT refers to a solution or component being unable to perform it's required functions to meet expectations and requirements. Failures in IT are inevitable, so it's important to plan for failures and design workloads to continue performing and meeting requirements when a component in the solution fails. Designing for failure in the AWS Cloud starts with ensuring each component of a workload has a redundant component in a different Availability Zone (AZ) ensuring each component can fail over to a healthy resource if one experiences a failure. Some AWS services include features to automatically deploy redundant resources in multiple AZ's, such as Amazon S3 and Amazon DynamoDB. Those services have built-in mechanisms to automatically fail over to a healthy resource if the resource servicing requests fails. Other services, like Amazon EC2, require customers to launch multiple resources and use AWS services, like Elastic Load Balancing or Auto Scaling, to distribute traffic across all components of a workload. When Elastic Load Balancing detects a failed component, it will cease sending traffic to the unhealthy resource and only distribute traffic across healthy resources. When Auto Scaling detects a failure, it will launch another resource to take the place of the unhealthy one. Designing for failure also includes monitoring the health of components and sending notifications when events impact the availability of a workload. Features of AWS Services, like Amazon CloudWatch Alarms, can be configured to trigger when a failure occurs. AWS customers can configure CloudWatch Alarms to send email notifications when failures occur or to integrate with Amazon SNS to log incidents in incident tracking systems.

Continue learning how customers can design for failure in the AWS Cloud by reading the Failure management, Design your workload to withstand component failures section of the Reliability Pillar - AWS Well-Architected Framework whitepaper.

Describe how customers can decouple components of a workload in the AWS Cloud

Monolithic architecture is a term that refers to an outdated way of developing systems and applications in which all components of a workload are combined into one resource or package. Developing monolithic architectures is not ideal in modern IT as all components in the architecture are dependent on each other decreasing the agility, flexibility, scalability, and reliability of the workload. If one component in a workload becomes unhealthy, the entire workload will experience a failure. Also, if one component needs to be updated, the entire workload must be taken offline to implement the change. Instead, workloads should be developed in the AWS Cloud by decoupling components making them independent of each other to improve the agility, flexibility, scalability, and reliability of the workload. To design and develop workloads with decoupled components, AWS customers can use a service-oriented architecture (SOA) in which components are developed independently and communicate with each other over a network using a common communication protocol. An example of an SOA in the AWS Cloud is several Amazon EC2 instances running different services of a distributed system with an Elastic Load Balancer distributing traffic across the instances in an Amazon VPC virtual private cloud. AWS customers can also decouple components of a workload using a variant of SOA called microservices architecture in which components are developed independent of each other in small, simple segments and communicate with each other using decoupling mechanisms, like API's and message queues and services, and notification services. An example of a microservices architecture in the AWS Cloud is several AWS Lambda functions running different modules of an application communicating with each other using decoupling mechanisms, such as Amazon API Gateway API's, Amazon SQS message queues, and Amazon SNS notifications.

Continue learning about how customers can decouple components of a workload in the AWS Cloud by reading the Workload architecture, Design your workload service architecture section of the Reliability Pillar - AWS Well-Architected Framework whitepaper.

Describe how customers can implement elasticity in the AWS cloud

The goal of elasticity is scalability and reliability of a workload. AWS offers many elastic, managed services that scale up and down automatically to meet demand. This level of scalability and reliability made possible by the elasticity of the AWS Cloud cannot be matched with on-premises infrastructure. Amazon S3 is an example of a storage service offered by AWS that scales up and down automatically by default to meet demand. As objects are stored in an S3 bucket, the AWS Cloud automatically provisions more resources to store the extra data. When objects are removed, the Cloud automatically removes resources that are no longer needed. AWS Lambda is another example of a compute service offered by AWS that scales automatically. When a Lambda function is invoked, the AWS Cloud automatically provisions the compute and memory resources to run the code in the function. When the function is finished executing, the resources are removed and available for the AWS Cloud to be provisioned for other resources. AWS also offers a service, AWS Auto Scaling, to automatically scale resources up and down to meet demand and ensure workloads remain healthy in order to meet expectations and requirements. AWS resources that can be scaled with AWS Auto Scaling include Amazon EC2 instances and Spot Fleets, Amazon ECS tasks, Amazon DynamoDB tables and indexes, and Amazon Aurora Replicas.

Continue learning about how customers can implement elasticity in the AWS Cloud by reading the Change management, Design your workload to adapt to changes in demand section of the Reliability Pillar - AWS Well-Architected Framework whitepaper.

Describe how customers can think parallel in the AWS Cloud

Thinking parallel in the AWS Cloud refers to designing workloads with multiple resources or resources that can handle multiple operations at once to optimize reliability and performance. Amazon Elastic Load Balancing (ELB) is one AWS service that optimizes both reliability and performance through parallelization of resources, like Amazon EC2 instances. When a workload is designed to use a load balancer to distribute requests across multiple resources in parallel, the load balancer will stop sending requests to any unhealthy resource and continue distributing requests amongst the healthy resources ensuring the workload is reliable and continues meeting requirements during a failure. ELB optimizes performance of a workload through parallelization by distributing requests across all healthy resources ensuring no resource gets overloaded with requests and the workload meets performance expectations. Amazon Elastic File System (EFS) is one AWS service that optimizes performance by handling multiple operations at once, or in parallel. Customers can connect thousands of EC2 instances to an EFS file system and service many parallel storage requests ensuring workloads meet performance expectations even when many instances request files at the same time.

Continue learning about how customers can think parallel to optimize reliability by reading the Failure management, Use fault isolation to protect your workload section of the Reliability Pillar - AWS Well-Architected Framework whitepaper. Continue learning about how customers can think parallel to optimize performance by reading the Selection, Storage Architecture Selection section of the Performance Efficiency Pillar - AWS Well-Architected Framework whitepaper.

Technology
Exam Domain

Define the methods of deploying and operating in the AWS Cloud

Create and activate an AWS account

To get started working in the AWS Cloud, customers must create and activate an AWS account. To create an AWS account, the customer visits the Amazon Web Services home page at aws.amazon.com and selects Create an AWS Account. The customer then enters their email address and desired account name and verifies their email address using a code sent to the email address they entered. After verifying their email address, the customer creates a password and selects which type of account they want to create, Personal or Business. The account types have the same features and functionality. The difference is the customer enters their personal information for a personal account during account creation, and they enter information about their company for a business account. When creating the account, in addition to the account name, email address, and password the customer must agree to the AWS Customer Agreement and enter a phone number, physical address, and credit or debit card number. After the credit or debit card number is entered, the customer must verify their account and payment information using a PIN sent to the phone number they entered. Finally, the customer selects an AWS Support Plan and they receive an email address stating their account has been activated. Once their account is activated, the customer can begin using AWS services and features.

Continue learning about creating and activating an AWS account by browsing the Create and activate an AWS account web page at aws.amazon.com/premiumsupport/knowledge-center/create-and-activate-aws-account/.

List the tools customers can use to access services in the AWS Cloud

AWS offers many tools for deploying, developing, and operating in the Cloud. However, there are three primary tools customers use to access AWS services to manage and deploy resources and develop applications in the AWS Cloud: the AWS Management Console (Web Console), the AWS Command Line Interface (CLI), and Software Development Kits (SDKs).

Continue learning about the tools customers can use to access AWS services by reading the Developer tools section of the AWS Cloud Essentials web page at aws.amazon.com/getting-started/cloud-essentials/.

Describe the AWS Management Console

The AWS Management Console is the graphical web interface AWS customers can use to create an account, view available services, purchase services, configure services, and perform almost any task to interact with the AWS Cloud. Customers can access the AWS Management Console using most Internet browsers. Once logged in, customers can navigate to the console of any service offered by AWS to view and manage resources hosted with the service. AWS also offers a mobile application that enables customers to sign in to their AWS account to view and manage their resources from their mobile device.

Continue learning about the AWS Management Console by reading the What is the AWS Management Console? section of the AWS Management Console Getting Started User Guide.

Describe the AWS Command Line Interface

The AWS Command Line Interface (CLI) is a tool enabling customers to manage and interact with their AWS services and resources using commands and scripts rather than navigating a graphical web interface. An AWS customer can install the CLI shell program on their own device running a supported Operating System. After installing and configuring the AWS CLI, a customer can use it to enter commands to manage and interact with their AWS services and resources and can run scripts to automate management tasks.

Continue learning about the AWS Command Line Interface by reading the About the AWS CLI section of the AWS Command Line Interface User Guide.

Describe the AWS Software Development Kits

A Software Development Kit (SDK) is a set of standardized tools a developer uses to write code and ensure the application components they develop can interact with other components, applications, and the platform they run on. AWS offers SDK's for supported development languages that can be downloaded from the AWS website. AWS developers use the AWS SDK's to develop applications in the AWS Cloud.

Continue learning about AWS SDKs and other developer tools by browsing the Tools to Build on AWS web page at aws.amazon.com/tools/.

Describe how customers can implement Infrastructure as Code in the AWS Cloud

Infrastructure as Code (IaC) is an IT practice in which infrastructure components are deployed and maintained automatically using code or software instead of being deployed and maintained manually. In IaC, infrastructure components are typically deployed collectively as one solution rather than deploying each component separately. AWS CloudFormation is an infrastructure as code orchestration service that enables customers to describe their infrastructure as code in order to automatically provision, deploy, modify, and update a collection of related AWS resources. With CloudFormation, a customer can create templates for their infrastructure from scratch or they can start from one of the CloudFormation sample templates. CloudFormation templates can be stored locally or in an S3 bucket. CloudFormation can be accessed via the Management Console, CLI, or APIs to deploy AWS resources from the customer's infrastructure as code template.

Continue learning about AWS CloudFormation by browsing the AWS CloudFormation web page at aws.amazon.com/cloudformation/.

Describe how customers can automate configuration management in the AWS Cloud

Configuration management is an IT practice in which consistent changes are made to a product or group of related products. The goal of configuration management is to ensure related components are configured the same way every time. To ensure changes are made consistently, change management processes are most often automated using code and tools, such as Chef and Puppet. AWS OpsWorks is a configuration management service that enables a customer to provision Chef and Puppet instances to automate configuring, deploying, and managing servers in the AWS Cloud and on-premises. Another service commonly used to automate configuration management in the AWS cloud is AWS Systems Manager. AWS Systems Manager stores the customer's infrastructure configuration in a central location enabling automation of configuration and policy changes across resources in their AWS and on-premises environment.

Continue learning about AWS OpsWorks by browsing the AWS OpsWorks web page at aws.amazon.com/opsworks/.

Describe how customers can implement source control in the AWS Cloud

Source control, also referred to as version control, revision control, or source code management, is an IT practice in which source code for a development project is tracked and managed with source control management systems, such as Git. AWS CodeCommit is a source control service that hosts Git-based repositories. CodeCommit enables AWS customers to store source code for applications built in the AWS Cloud and on-premises. AWS customers can track and manage changes to source code, manage user access to repositories, and integrate existing Git tools with CodeCommit.

Continue learning about AWS CodeCommit by browsing the AWS CodeCommit web page at aws.amazon.com/codecommit/.

Describe how customers can automate software deployment in the AWS Cloud

Deploying software automatically ensures the software can be deployed by anybody, it can be deployed at any time, it can be deployed multiple times, and it can always be deployed in the same way eliminating user error. AWS Elastic Beanstalk is a software deployment service that enables customers to automatically deploy web applications and services on web servers, such as Apache, Nginx, Passenger, and Microsoft IIS. Elastic Beanstalk automates capacity provisioning, load balancing, auto-scaling, and health monitoring for applications and services deployed on web servers. AWS CodeDeploy is a software deployment service that enables customers to automate deployment of software to Amazon EC2 instances, AWS Fargate containers, AWS Lambda functions, and on-premises servers. Customers can deploy the same applications consistently in development, test, and production environments seamlessly across the AWS Cloud and on-premises platforms with CodeDeploy.

Continue learning about AWS Elastic Beanstalk by browsing the AWS Elastic Beanstalk web page at aws.amazon.com/elasticbeanstalk/. Continue learning about AWS CodeDeploy by browsing the AWS CodeDeploy web page at aws.amazon.com/codedeploy/.

Describe how customers can implement continuous delivery in the AWS Cloud

Releasing custom applications in an enterprise IT environment is a process that begins after the code is written starting with building the software, then testing it, and finally delivering it to a staging environment for approval before it is deployed to the production environment. Continuous delivery is a practice that automates the release process, often referred to as a release pipeline, all the way from building the software to delivering it to the staging environment. AWS CodePipeline is a continuous delivery service that automates the release pipeline for application and infrastructure updates. With CodePipeline, a customer creates a release pipeline to automatically build and test an application or infrastructure when changes are made to the source code. The release pipeline can be configured to automatically deploy the updated application or infrastructure to the production environment if all tests are successful. Alternately, the pipeline can be configured to require manual approval to deploy the application or infrastructure to the production environment.

Continue learning about AWS CodePipeline by browsing the AWS CodePipeline web page at aws.amazon.com/codepipeline/.

Describe how customers can implement containers in the AWS Cloud

A container is a self-contained application that is packaged together with all dependencies the application needs to function, such as the source code, binary data files, and configuration files. Unlike traditional applications, containers are not installed on the computing platform or operating system. Instead, containers run on a container platform, such as Docker, independently of the operating system. This results in meeting two major goals of containerization: 1) containerized applications can run on almost any environment, such as on-premises servers and cloud platforms, and 2) developers can use containers to develop applications with little to no knowledge of any underlying operating system. AWS offers two container orchestration services to provide a container platform to customers, Amazon Elastic Container Service (ECS) and Amazon Elastic Kubernetes Service (EKS). ECS is a container service enabling customers to build, deploy, and manage containerized applications with Docker in the AWS Cloud. ECS containers can be launched as Amazon EC2 container instances or AWS Fargate serverless containers. EKS is a Kubernetes container orchestration service enabling customers to provision Kubernetes clusters with AWS Fargate serverless compute engine or Amazon EC2. Launching serverless containers with AWS Fargate ensures customers don't have to manage underlying infrastructure. With AWS Fargate, customers can specify the resources required by their containers, such as CPU and memory, and AWS Fargate handles the rest, including launching the containers, scaling the containers, and managing the availability of the containers.

Continue learning about Amazon ECS by browsing the Amazon ECS web page at aws.amazon.com/ecs/. Continue learning about Amazon EKS by browsing the Amazon EKS web page at aws.amazon.com/eks/. Continue learning about AWS Fargate by browsing the AWS Fargate web page at aws.amazon.com/fargate/.

Describe how customers can implement hybrid cloud with AWS

Hybrid cloud is a cloud deployment model in which customers integrate their on-premises environments with their public cloud environments. AWS customers commonly implement hybrid cloud solutions in order to extend AWS services on-premises, extend their data centers to the AWS Cloud, and seamlessly migrate workloads and data between their on-premises and AWS environments. AWS offers hybrid cloud services enabling customers to migrate workloads and data between environments for use cases such as ensuring business continuity during disasters, placing applications and data closer to global users, extending capacity to meet increases in demand, and taking advantage of the capabilities and features of AWS services on-premises. AWS Outposts is a family of hybrid cloud services that enable customers to launch AWS infrastructure and services in their on-premises environments. With Outposts, AWS delivers physical hardware to customer's data center to be installed by AWS, the customer's personnel, or third-party vendors. After the hardware is installed and powered on, the AWS services supported by Outposts are automatically provisioned on the hardware enabling customers to launch AWS resources in their data center. Other common AWS hybrid cloud services and use cases include VMware Cloud on AWS enabling VMware workloads to migrate between AWS and on-premises environments, AWS Storage Gateway enabling on-premises workloads to use AWS storage, and AWS Direct Connect enabling on-premises networks to connect to Amazon virtual private clouds.

Continue learning about the hybrid cloud services AWS offers by browsing the AWS Hybrid Cloud web page at aws.amazon.com/hybrid/.

Describe how customers can deploy machine learning models in the AWS Cloud

Machine learning is a branch of artificial intelligence in which developers build algorithms and statistical models to train applications to perform tasks they are not explicitly programmed to perform. Machine learning is the science behind common applications and machines that perform human-like activities, like chatbots, predictive text, language translation apps, search engine recommendations, and autonomous vehicles. Data scientists and business analysts often use machine learning models to analyze data and predict future outcomes. Amazon SageMaker is a machine learning service that enables customers to build, train, and deploy machine learning models in the AWS Cloud. With SageMaker, customers can use built-in data wrangling translations to fetch data from multiple data sources, clean the data to make it consistent, and prepare the data to train their machine learning models. Customers can use pre-built machine learning models or build their own model with SageMaker and use the prepared data to train the model to perform the desired tasks. Once a model is trained, customers can easily deploy the model and seamlessly integrate it into their existing applications.

Continue learning about Amazon SageMaker by browsing the Amazon SageMaker web page at aws.amazon.com/sagemaker/.

Describe how customers can run batch computing jobs in the AWS Cloud

Batch processing, often called batch computing, is a method of using compute resources to run multiple data related tasks, called jobs, automatically without user interaction. Organizations use batch processing to analyze large amounts of data efficiently for use cases and tasks that would otherwise take too much time or could not be completed manually, such as analyzing large amounts of financial data to make predictions on future market performance. AWS Batch is a batch processing service that enables customers to easily run hundreds of thousands of batch computing jobs in the AWS Cloud. With AWS Batch, customers do not need to provision compute resources manually. Instead, customers configure the minimum and desired specifications for the compute environment where their batch computing jobs will run. Then, customers submit their jobs to a job queue where they sit until it is their turn to run in the environment. As the jobs in the queue run, AWS Batch automatically launches the compute resources needed to run and complete each job. There is no additional charge to customers to use AWS Batch beyond the charge to run the compute resources and store the batch computing jobs in their AWS environment.

Continue learning about AWS Batch by browsing the AWS Batch web page at aws.amazon.com/batch/.

Describe how customers can migrate data to the AWS Cloud

AWS offers many services and solutions to help customers migrate data to the AWS Cloud. Which option customers choose depends on the type and amount of data being moved, the network resources available to move the data, how users will access the data after it's moved, and many other considerations that must be taken into account. AWS offers both online and offline solutions to migrate data to the Cloud. Online solutions use resources to efficiently migrate data over a network, whereas offline solutions require hardware devices to be shipped back and forth between the customer and AWS to transfer data to the Cloud. AWS DataSync is an online data migration service enabling customers to transfer object and file data to AWS over a network with automated workflows. With DataSync, customers can migrate data from their on-premises environment to Amazon S3, EFS, FSx for Windows File Servers, and FSx for Lustre using AWS Direct Connect to encrypt online data transfer. DataSync can also be used to migrate data between AWS object and file storage services for replication and archiving purposes or to share application data. The AWS Snow Family is a family of offline data migration devices enabling customers to migrate block and object data to AWS without the use of network resources. The Snow Family consists of three different devices, AWS Snowcone, Snowball, and Snowmobile. Snowcone is the small device in the Snow Family, and each device is capable of storing and transferring 8 TB of data to the AWS Cloud. Snowball is a medium sized device capable of storing and transferring 42TB of data. Both Snowcone and Snowball devices are shipped from AWS to the customer via a courier service and are shipped back to AWS from the customer after data is loaded onto the device. Snowmobile is the largest member of the Snow Family. Each Snowmobile device is capable of storing and transferring up to 100PB of data to the AWS Cloud. Snowmobile devices arrive at a customer's site in a shipping container pulled by a semi-trailer truck. After data is loaded onto the Snowmobile device, the shipping container is pulled back to AWS to upload the data to the Cloud.

Continue learning about the data migration service and solutions offered by AWS by browsing the Cloud Data Migration on AWS web page at aws.amazon.com/cloud-data-migration/.

Describe Amazon API Gateway

An Application Programming Interface (API) is code built to enable application components and services to communicate with each other in order to share data or functionality. Amazon API Gateway is a service that enables customers to build, deploy, and manage APIs to enable their front end client applications to access to their AWS resources and data stored in the Cloud. APIs built and deployed with API Gateway can act as a front door for clients to access compute resources, such as an AWS Lambda function, storage resources, such as an Amazon S3 bucket, and many other resources hosted in the AWS Cloud. AWS developers can build REST, HTTP, and WebSocket API's in API Gateway and deploy them in their own AWS environment or package and sell them as a Software-as-a-Service product in the AWS Marketplace.

Continue learning about Amazon API Gateway by browsing the Amazon API Gateway web page at aws.amazon.com/api-gateway/.

Describe Amazon SQS

A message queue in computer science is a communication mechanism that enables application components and services to communicate with each other by sharing messages. With message queue services, messages are placed in the queue by the source component, called the producer. The messages remain in the queue until they are removed and processed by the destination component, called the consumer.

Messages in a queue can be anything the producer needs to share with the consumer, such as requests for the consumer to perform a process, error messages for the consumer to send to an administrator, or simply information to share with the consumer. Amazon Simple Queue Service (SQS) is a message queue service enabling customers to build decoupled and scalable microservices, distributed systems, and serverless applications in the AWS Cloud. With SQS, customers can create queues to enable inter-process communication between their application components and services to share requests, replies, error messages, or any other information required for the functionality of the solution. The benefits of using Amazon SQS include automatic scaling of message queues to handle any amount of traffic, support for multiple message producers and consumers, and built-in redundancy to ensure high availability of messages.

Continue learning about Amazon SQS by browsing the Amazon SQS web page at aws.amazon.com/sqs/.

Describe Amazon SNS

Amazon Simple Notification Service (SNS) is a messaging service that enables application-to-application (A2A) and application-to-person (A2P) communication in the AWS Cloud. SNS is commonly used as a decoupling mechanism to modernize applications and systems in the AWS Cloud by breaking them into smaller, independent components. With SNS, customers can create a topic to act as a communication channel between application components and services in decoupled and scalable microservices, distributed systems, and serverless applications. AWS resources can be configured as publishers, or producers, to send messages to a topic. Client applications can subscribe to a topic and receive messages from the publisher via SMS, email, mobile push notifications, or a supported AWS service, such as Amazon SQS, Kinesis Firehose, or AWS Lambda. Subscribers to the topic are often referred to as consumers.

Continue learning about Amazon SNS by browsing the Amazon SNS web page at aws.amazon.com/sns/.

Describe AWS Athena

AWS Athena is a query service that enables customers to gather and analyze data from Amazon S3, CloudFront, CloudTrail, and many other supported AWS services. Athena is a fully managed service ensuring customers don't have to manage any underlying infrastructure or operating systems to gather and analyze their data. With Athena, customers can easily connect to their supported AWS resources to begin querying data from the resources using standard SQL queries. Athena can be used to generate reports or explore data with business intelligence tools or SQL clients. Athena can also integrate with Amazon QuickSight enabling customers to visualize data gathered by Athena and other sources in a single dashboard.

Continue learning about Amazon Athena by browsing the Amazon Athena web page at aws.amazon.com/athena/.

Describe Amazon Kinesis

Streaming data is data that is continuously generated by many data sources and is simultaneously sent to storage media or applications for processing and analysis. Examples of streaming data includes log files generated by applications, financial data generated by ecommerce, marketing and personal data generated by social networks, and streaming videos generated by surveillance systems. Amazon Kinesis is a platform of services that enable customers to collect, process, and analyze streaming data to provide insights into their data and environment. Amazon Kinesis consists of four streaming data services: Kinesis Video Streams, Data Streams, Data Firehose, and Data Analytics. Video Streams is a service enabling customers to stream live video to the AWS Cloud from any device, such as smartphones, security cameras, webcams, and drones. With Video Streams, customers can store streaming videos securely, view video in real time, and build applications for video processing and analytics. Kinesis Data Streams is a service that enables customers to stream data to the AWS Cloud and create data-processing applications to read the data and send processed records to dashboards, generate alerts, make dynamic changes to live data and applications, and gain insights into the status and functionality of their environment.

Continue learning about Amazon Kinesis by browsing the Amazon Kinesis web page at aws.amazon.com/kinesis/.

AWS Transit Gateway

AWS Transit Gateway is a networking resource customers can use to simplify connecting their virtual private clouds (VPCs) to each other and on-premises networks using a single gateway and the secure AWS global network. As a customer's AWS environment grows, they may have multiple VPCs connected to each other with VPC peering or other networking features, and they may have VPCs connected to multiple on-premises networks using AWS Direct Connect, VPNs, or other AWS connectivity resources. As an environment grows, it can become increasingly difficult to manage and monitor the various networks and connectivity resources deployed. Transit Gateway simplifies managing and monitoring various networks with a hub and spoke model ensuring customers only have to connect their VPCs and AWS connectivity resources to the Transit Gateway instead of each other to enable communication between multiple VPC's and on-premises networks. AWS Transit Gateway supports both IPv4 and IPv6 traffic, can connect up to 5,000 VPCs and VPN connections, and supports routing for multiple types of protocols, including Border Gateway Protocol (BGP) and Open Shortest Path First (OSPF).

Continue learning about AWS Transit Gateway by browsing the AWS Transit Gateway web page at aws.amazon.com/transit-gateway/.

Describe AWS Direct Connect

AWS Direct Connect is a cloud connectivity service enabling customers to configure communication between their on-premises networks and their VPC's in the AWS Cloud. Direct Connect establishes a direct network connection between on-premises networks and one or more VPC's within the same AWS Region. The direct network connection allows traffic between on-premises resources and resources in the AWS Cloud to bypass the Internet where traffic patterns can vary widely resulting in unpredictable performance. Direct Connect connectivity occurs over high speed ethernet fiber-optic hardware ensuring extremely low network latency and high throughput that is typically not achievable with other Network-to-Amazon VPC connectivity options, such as AWS Managed VPN.

Continue learning about AWS Direct Connect by reading the What is AWS Direct Connect section of the AWS Direct Connect User Guide.

Describe AWS Service Quotas

AWS enforces limits, called service quotas, on how many resources a customer can consume with each AWS service. If a customer reaches the limit of the service quota, they will not be able to provision any more resources with the service. AWS Service Quotas is an interface that enables customers to view their service quotas, view their current utilization of resources, request a service quota increase, and configure CloudWatch alarms to notify them when they are nearing the limit of their service quota. The Service Quotas interface can be accessed using the AWS Management Console for a graphical user interface, the AWS CLI, or with applications built with AWS SDKs.

Continue learning about AWS Service Quotas by reading the What is Service Quotas? section of the Service Quotas User Guide.

Describe AWS Systems Manager

AWS Systems Manager is an operations service enabling customers to gain insight into the operational status and automate operational tasks across AWS and on-premises infrastructure resources. Systems Manager includes five capability categories to simplify operations for different use cases: Operations Management, Application Management, Change Management, Node Management, and Shared Resources. Operations Management capabilities help customers manage their AWS resources to mitigate and recover from incidents, visual operational data and patch compliance, and view, investigate, and resolve operational work items. Application Management capabilities help customers manage their applications running in the AWS Cloud by investigating and resolving issues with resources hosting application components, create, manage, and deploy application configurations, and securely store configuration data and manage secrets. The Change Management capabilities help customers manage changes to their AWS resources hosting their applications. With Change Management, customers can request, approve, implement, report on, schedule, and automate operational changes to their applications and resources. The Node Management capabilities help customers manage their Amazon EC2 instances, edge devices, and on-premises servers and virtual machines in a hybrid cloud environment. The Shared Resources capabilities enable customers to use a Systems Manager document (SSM document) to manage and configure their AWS resources automatically in large scale AWS environments.

Continue learning about AWS Systems Manager by browsing the AWS Systems Manager web page at aws.amazon.com/systems-manager/.

Define the AWS global infrastructure

List the primary components of the AWS Global Infrastructure

The AWS Global Infrastructure is the network of infrastructure hardware, software, and data centers that host the AWS Cloud across the world. The AWS Global Infrastructure is comprised of two primary components that make AWS services available to customers: Regions and Availability Zones. Other components of the AWS Global Infrastructure include Local Zones, edge locations, and regional edge caches.

Continue learning about the primary components of the AWS Global Infrastructure by reading the Global Infrastructure section of the Overview of Amazon Web Services whitepaper.

Describe AWS Regions

An AWS Region is a geographic location where AWS has physical data centers to provide services to AWS customers. AWS has Regions across the world, and each AWS account has access to all Regions available in the AWS Cloud. When a customer launches a resource in AWS, they first select which Region they want the resource to reside in. AWS has Regions around the world ensuring the resources launched and operated by customers are close to their users and applications to reduce network latency and provide optimal performance. Each Region consists of at least three Availability Zones to ensure redundancy and reliability of AWS resources. AWS Regions operate independently from each other. However, they are interconnected and customers can replicate or migrate resources across Regions using various AWS services and features.

Continue learning about AWS Regions by reading the Regions section on the Global Infrastructure Regions & AZs web page at aws.amazon.com/about-aws/global-infrastructure/regions_az/.

Describe AWS Availability Zones

An AWS Availability Zone (AZ) is a physically isolated data center or cluster of data centers in an AWS Region. By physically isolating each AZ, AWS ensures a failure in one AZ does not impact any other AZs. Each Region has multiple AZs separated geographically and interconnected with private, high-bandwidth, low-latency networking. All AZs have redundant power, cooling, compute, storage, and networking ensuring resiliency and redundancy within the data center. When AWS customers launch a virtual private cloud (VPC), the VPC spans all AZs in the Region by default. However, customers can customize their VPC by selecting how many AZs they want the VPC to span and by creating subnets in different AZs to further control which AZ resources in the subnet will reside in. Launching clustered or redundant resources in different Availability Zones increases fault tolerance and availability of workloads in the AWS Cloud.

Continue learning about AWS Availability Zones by reading the Availability Zones section on the Global Infrastructure & AZs web page at aws.amazon.com/about-aws/global-infrastructure/regions_az/.

Describe AWS Local Zones

An AWS Local Zone is a data center or cluster of data centers in an AWS Region similar to an Availability Zone. AWS Local Zones are located in cities that have a high concentration of AWS customers, such as Los Angeles and New York City (New Jersey). Resources hosted with compute, storage, database, and other core AWS services can be launched in Local Zones to bring them closer to end-users and applications. Launching resources in Local Zones helps customers optimize performance of applications requiring single-digit millisecond latency and improve user experience.

Continue learning about AWS Local Zones by browsing the AWS Local Zones web page at aws.amazon.com/about-aws/global-infrastructure/localzones/.

Describe CloudFront edge locations

A CloudFront edge location is a physical site in the Global Infrastructure that Amazon CloudFront content delivery networks use to cache, or temporarily store, copies of content frequently accessed by users and applications. By caching frequently accessed content in edge locations, CloudFront ensures faster delivery of the content to meet the needs of users and applications. Edge locations are typically found in major cities with high populations of AWS users.

Continue learning about CloudFront edge locations by reading the Global Edge Network section on the Key Features of a Content Delivery Network web page at aws.amazon.com/cloudfront/features/.

Describe CloudFront regional edge caches

A CloudFront regional edge cache is a type of edge location with a larger cache and the ability to store more content for a longer period of time. The purpose of a regional edge cache is similar to that of an edge location. Amazon CloudFront content delivery networks temporarily store copies of frequently accessed content in a regional edge cache to provide faster delivery of the content to the user or application. Regional edge caches are not available in all AWS Regions.

Continue learning about CloudFront regional edge caches by reading How CloudFront works with regional edge caches in the What is Amazon CloudFront?, How CloudFront delivers content section of the Amazon CloudFront Developer Guide.

Identify how many Regions the AWS Cloud is available in

AWS regularly adds Regions to the Global Infrastructure. As of 2022, the AWS Cloud operates in 26 Regions globally. To find out how many Regions the AWS Cloud currently operates in, visit the AWS website and search for Global Infrastructure to find a page that summarizes the number of components in the AWS Global Infrastructure.

Continue learning about how many Regions AWS operates in and those that are announced and coming soon by browsing the Global Infrastructure web page at aws.amazon.com/about-aws/global-infrastructure/.

Identify how many Availability Zones the AWS Cloud spans

AWS regularly adds Availability Zones to the Global Infrastructure. As of 2022, the AWS Cloud operates in 84 Availability Zones globally. To find out how many Availability Zones the AWS Cloud currently operates in, visit the AWS website and search for Global Infrastructure to find a page that summarizes the number of components in the AWS Global Infrastructure.

Continue learning about how many Availability Zones AWS operates in by browsing the Global Infrastructure web page at aws.amazon.com/about-aws/global-infrastructure/.

Determine which Region to host AWS Cloud resources

When customers choose a Region to launch an AWS Cloud resource, they should consider and find the balance between three key factors: location, cost, and compliance requirements. Customers should consider Regions that are closest to the users and applications that will most often access the resource. The further away from the resource a user resides, the more likely they are to experience performance issues resulting in slow response time from the resource. Customers should also research, test, and estimate the cost of operating resources in each Region. The cost of hosting resources will be different for each Region due to many factors, such as the price AWS pays to purchase or import technologies into the Region and the differing price AWS pays to operate the Global Infrastructure in the Region. Customers should research each Region they are considering to host their infrastructure and applications to ensure they will comply with any laws, policies, and regulations required in the Region, such as GDPR, PCI-DSS, or HIPAA. To summarize the balance customers must find between the factors to consider when choosing a Region, they should launch their AWS resources in the closest Region to their users and applications, with the lowest cost they can afford, in which they can comply with relevant laws, policies, and regulations.

Continue learning about choosing a Region to host AWS Cloud resources by reading Choose your workload's location based on network requirements in the Selection, Network Architecture Selection section of the Performance Efficiency Pillar - AWS Well-Architected Framework whitepaper.

Determine which Availability Zone to host AWS Cloud resources

Availability Zones (AZs) help AWS customers achieve high availability and fault tolerance when operating in the AWS Cloud. Each AZ is a separate data center or group of data centers with no single point of failure within a Region. If high availability or fault tolerance is the goal, this can be accomplished by launching identical AWS resources in more than one AZ. The resources can be clustered together into one solution, or they can be used in a primary and backup configuration where the primary resource is used in production, and the backup is failed over to if the primary resource experiences a failure or service disruption.

Continue learning about choosing an Availability Zone to host AWS Cloud resources by reading Single AWS Region in the Disaster recovery is different in the cloud section of the Disaster Recovery of Workloads on AWS: Recovery in the AWS Cloud whitepaper.

Describe the role AWS Regions play in disaster recovery

Deploying resources and backing up data in multiple Availability Zones (AZs) within a Region is typically sufficient to recover from most disasters that may occur. However, AZs within a Region may be in close proximity to each other, and natural disasters or technical disasters, such as a loss of power grid resources, may impact multiple AZs or even an entire Region. To protect mission-critical applications and data from natural or technical disasters that impact an entire Region, it is recommended to back up or replicate the applications and data to another AWS Region.

Continue learning about the role AWS Regions play in disaster recovery by reading Multiple AWS Regions in the Disaster recovery is different in the cloud section of the Disaster Recovery of Workloads on AWS: Recovery in the AWS Cloud whitepaper.

Describe AWS Global Accelerator

AWS Global Accelerator is a networking service enabling customers to utilize the AWS global network to reduce network hops and improve performance of user and web application traffic by up to 60%. With Global Accelerator, customers create an accelerator and add listeners to process inbound connections from users and client applications. Customers add endpoints to an accelerator where the accelerator will send traffic from inbound connections. Examples of common endpoints include EC2 instances that host back-end applications and services and Application Load Balancers that distribute traffic across compute resources.

Continue learning about AWS Global Accelerator by browsing the AWS Global Accelerator web page at aws.amazon.com/global-accelerator/.

Describe AWS Wavelength

AWS Wavelength is an edge computing service enabling customers to build ultra-low latency applications in Wavelength Zones where they are accessible by 5G mobile devices. A Wavelength Zone is a physical site in an AWS Region deployed in a location close to telecommunication carriers' 5G networks. Customers can deploy Amazon EC2 instances running applications in Wavelength Zones to ensure the applications are close to carrier networks and can achieve peak performance. To ensure resources and applications are deployed in a Wavelength Zone, customers must opt in to Wavelength Zones with Amazon EC2. Then, they must create a new virtual private cloud or configure an existing one with a subnet and carrier gateway in a Wavelength Zone. When customers launch EC2 instances running applications in the subnet, the instances will be created in the Wavelength Zone ensuring the applications are close to telecommunication carriers' 5G networks.

Continue learning about AWS Wavelength by browsing the 5G Edge Computing Infrastructure - AWS Wavelength web page at aws.amazon.com/wavelength/.

Identify the core AWS services

Describe Amazon EC2

Amazon EC2 (Elastic Compute Cloud) is a compute service enabling customers to launch compute instances in order to host applications and services in the AWS Cloud. An EC2 instance is a virtual computing environment comparable to a virtual machine (VM), or virtual server. An instance has virtual hardware similar to a VM, such as vCPUs, memory, and storage, and has an installed operating system, such as Microsoft Windows or Linux. When launching an EC2 instance, a customer first selects an Amazon Machine Image (AMI) which serves as a template with the pre-installed Operating System and software the customer wants for their instance. Next, the customer selects the instance type which is a predetermined configuration of virtual hardware. Each instance type is designed for common use cases. For example, compute optimized instances include more vCPUs and can process data and requests faster than most other instance types. Amazon EC2 offers five instance types: general purpose, compute optimized, accelerated computing, memory optimized, and storage optimized. Within each instance type, there are instance families, such as Mac, T, M, and A instance families within the general purpose instance type. Within each instance family, there are generations which are slight variations in configurations. Within each instance generation, there are sizes, such as small, medium, and large. The instance family and generation determine the hardware and features available to the instance, such as Intel Core i7 processors. The instance size determines how much of each resource is available to the instance, such as 32GB of memory.

Continue learning about Amazon EC2 by browsing the Amazon EC2 web page at aws.amazon.com/ec2/.

Identify use cases for EC2 general purpose instances

General purpose instances include a balance of compute, memory, storage, and networking capacity. General purpose instances are optimized for workloads that do not require the use of any one of these resources more than the others. Examples of ideal use cases for general purpose instances include development environments, web servers, containerized microservices, virtual desktops, and small to medium sized databases. The families within the general purpose instance type are Mac, T, M, and A, and the generations are Mac, T4g, T3, T3a, T2, M6g, M6i, M6a, M5, M5a, M5n M5zn, M4, and A1.

Continue learning about EC2 general purpose instance use cases by reading about each instance family in the Instances, Instance types, General purpose section of the Amazon Elastic Compute Cloud User Guide for Linux Instances.

Identify use cases for EC2 compute optimized instances

Compute optimized instances are backed by high performance processers and are optimized for CPU intensive applications and workloads that require high-performing compute capacity. Examples of ideal use cases for compute optimized instances include high performance computing, media transcoding, batch processing workloads, gaming servers, and ad serving. The families within the compute optimized instance type are C and Hpc, and the generations are C7g, C6g, C6gn, C6i, C6a, C5, C5a, C5n, C4, and Hpc6a.

Continue learning about EC2 compute optimized instance use cases by reading about each instance family in the Instances, Instance types, Compute optimized section of the Amazon Elastic Compute Cloud User Guide for Linux Instances.

Identify use cases for EC2 memory optimized instances

Memory optimized instances include high performing memory and are optimized for workloads that process large data sets in running memory. Examples of ideal use cases for memory optimized instances include open-source databases, in-memory databases, in-memory caches, and real-time big data analytics. The families within the compute optimized instance type are X, R, and z, and the generations are R6g, R6i, R5, R5a, R5b, R5n, R4, X2gd, X2idn, X2iedn, X2iezn, X1e, X1, High Memory, and z1d.

Continue learning about EC2 memory optimized instance use cases by reading about each instance family in the Instances, Instance types, Memory optimized section of the Amazon Elastic Compute Cloud User Guide for Linux Instances.

Identify use cases for EC2 storage optimized instances

Storage optimized instances provide high disk throughput and are optimized for I/O intensive workloads that require access to local storage. Examples of ideal use cases for storage optimized instances include NoSQL databases, distributed computing, scale-out transactional databases, data warehousing, log processing applications, and analytics workloads. The families within the storage optimized instance type are I, D, and H, and the generations are Im4gn, Is4gen, I4i, I3, I3en, D2, D3, D3en, and H1.

Continue learning about EC2 storage optimized instance use cases by reading about each instance family in the Instances, Instance types, Storage optimized section of the Amazon Elastic Compute Cloud User Guide for Linux Instances.

Identify use cases for EC2 accelerated computing instances

Accelerated computing instances are GPU based instances that are optimized for workloads that use hardware accelerators for massively parallel processing such as graphics processing or data pattern matching. Examples of ideal use cases for accelerated computing instances include training machine learning models, high performance computing, speech recognition, autonomous vehicles, molecular modeling, advanced text analysis, and server-side video rendering. The families within the accelerated computing instance type are P, DL, Trn, Inf, G, F, and VT, and the generations are P4, P3, P2, DL1, Trn1, Inf1, G5, G5g G4dn, G4ad, G3, F1, and VT1.

Continue learning about EC2 accelerated computing instance use cases by browsing the Accelerated Computing section of the Amazon EC2 Instance Types web page at aws.amazon.com/ec2/instance-types/#Accelerated_Computing.

Describe an Amazon Machine Image

An Amazon Machine Image (AMI) is a base configuration for EC2 instances that acts as a template when launching an instance. Each AMI is preconfigured with an operating system, installed software, and other customizations enabling customers to quickly launch an instance with the software configuration they need for their use case. The first step when launching an EC2 instance is to choose an AMI. Customers can choose AMIs created by AWS, custom AMIs they've created themselves, AMIs from other accounts, community AMIs other members of the AWS community have created, or AMIs available in the AWS Marketplace. The AWS Marketplace includes free AMIs as well as subscription-based AMIs that will be billed to the customer based on usage. It is a common practice for customers to launch an EC2 instance, configure the instance with a configuration commonly found in their AWS environment, and save the updated configuration as a custom AMI. When the customer needs an instance to start with the updated configuration, they can launch one from the AMI and the instance will include any software installed or customizations made before saving the AMI.

Continue learning about Amazon Machine Images by reading the Instances, Instances and AMIs section of the Amazon Elastic Compute Cloud User Guide for Linux Instances.

Describe an elastic network interface

An elastic network interface (ENI) is a virtual network card in a VPC. In the AWS Management Console and much of the AWS documentation, an ENI is simply referred to as a network interface. Using the Management Console, AWS CLI, or AWS Tools for Windows PowerShell, customers can create an ENI, select the subnet it should reside in, and configure it's private IP address. After an ENI is created, customers can attach it to an EC2 instance in the same Availability Zone where the

ENIs subnet resides. When the ENI is attached, the instance will inherit the private IP address and reside in the ENIs subnet. To enable Internet communication and assign a public IP address to an ENI and any EC2 instance it is attached to, customers can assign an Elastic IP address to the ENI. Each EC2 instance can have two or more ENIs attached depending on the instance size. However, each ENI can only be attached to one instance. Customers can quickly detach an ENI from an instance and attach it to another instance to ensure any traffic sent to the IP address of the ENI will go to the newly attached instance.

Continue learning elastic network interfaces by reading the Networking, Network interfaces section of the Amazon Elastic Compute Cloud User Guide for Linux Instances.

Describe an elastic IP address

An elastic IP address (EIP) is a static, public IP address customers can associate with any instance or network interface in their VPC. Before associating an EIP with an instance or interface, customers must allocate the EIP to their AWS account. They can do this by adding an IP address range they already own to their account or by allocating an EIP from a range of addresses owned by AWS. When an EIP is associated with an instance, the instance retains the IP address until the EIP is disassociated from the instance. AWS does not charge customers for the first EIP associated with a running instance, but customers will be charged for any additional EIPs associated with the instance. AWS charges a small hourly fee for any EIP that is not associated with an instance or interface and any EIP that is associated with a stopped instance or unattached interface. When an EIP is no longer needed, customers can release it from their account to ensure no fees are charged.

Continue learning about Elastic IP Addresses by reading the Networking, Elastic IP addresses section of the Amazon Elastic Compute Cloud User Guide for Linux Instances.

Describe an EC2 instance store

An instance store provides temporary, high-performance block storage for EC2 instances. Customers can configure an instance store for an EC2 instance only when the instance is created. Instance stores are commonly used to store data that changes frequently such as buffers, caches, and scratch data. When an instance is rebooted or stopped either purposely or due to a failure, the data stored in an instance store is lost. Therefore, valuable, long-term data for EC2 instances should never be stored in an instance store. Instead, the data that must be retained for an instance should be stored in durable storage solutions, like an EBS volume, EFS file system, or S3 bucket.

Continue learning about EC2 instance stores by reading the Storage, Instance store section of the Amazon Elastic Compute Cloud User Guide for Linux Instances.

Describe Amazon ECS

A container is a packaged application that includes the application code and all of its dependencies. Containers provide applications with everything the application needs in order to function ensuring the application can run on any computing environment and can be migrated from one environment to another. Amazon ECS (Elastic Container Service) is a container orchestration service enabling customers to deploy, manage, and scale Docker containers and containerized applications in the AWS Cloud. Customers can choose two launch types for their ECS containers: Fargate and EC2. The Fargate launch type enables containers to run in a serverless environment removing the customer's burden of managing infrastructure. ECS containers launched with Fargate are ideal for large workloads that need to be optimized for low overhead, small workloads that have occasional bursts in compute or memory usage, tiny workloads, and batch workloads. The EC2 launch type enables containers to run on EC2 instances allowing customers to have more control over the infrastructure hosting their applications. ECS containers launched with EC2 are ideal for workloads that require consistently high compute or memory usage, large workloads that need to be optimized for price, and applications that require access to persistent storage.

Continue learning about Amazon ECS by browsing the Amazon ECS web page at aws.amazon.com/ecs/.

Describe AWS Auto Scaling

AWS Auto Scaling is a resource scaling service enabling customers to automatically adjust capacity of supported AWS resources and achieve elasticity in the AWS Cloud. Auto Scaling is supported for Amazon EC2 instances and Spot Fleets, ECS tasks, DynamoDB tables and indexes, and Aurora replicas. With Auto Scaling, customers can use one of three built-in scaling strategies to optimize availability and performance, optimize cost, or both. When customers choose a built-in strategy, AWS automatically creates the scaling plan with predefined metrics. Alternately, customers can create a custom scaling strategy and manually configure the metrics in the scaling plan to determine when to increase or decrease capacity. Auto Scaling is offered to customers at no additional charge beyond the usage cost of scalable AWS resources, such as EC2 instances.

Continue learning about AWS Auto Scaling by browsing the AWS Auto Scaling web page at aws.amazon.com/autoscaling/.

Describe AWS Lambda

Serverless computing is a cloud computing architecture in which cloud services automatically provision compute resources an application needs to run, such as CPU and memory, independently without the need of a server or instance. AWS Lambda is a serverless compute service enabling customers to run applications and backend services without deploying, operating, and maintaining servers. With AWS Lambda, customers upload their existing code to Lambda as a function or they develop new code as functions using Lambda tools in the AWS Cloud. When customers create a function, they configure settings like the virtual private cloud the function will use if it requires network access and concurrency to determine how many instances of the function can run at the same time to meet demand. Customers can invoke their Lambda functions to run manually using the Lambda API. Alternately, functions can be configured to trigger and run automatically based on activity from other AWS services, HTTP endpoints, or in-app activity. When a trigger is set off, Lambda provisions the necessary compute resources and runs the function in multiple Availability Zones to ensure the function can still process events if a service disruption should occur. When the function ends, Lambda returns the resources back to the pool of resources available to the AWS Cloud.

Continue learning about AWS Lambda by browsing the AWS Lambda web page at aws.amazon.com/lambda/.

Describe Amazon Lightsail

Amazon Lightsail is a compute service enabling customers to quickly deploy virtual private servers, called instances, that are already configured with storage, networking, database engines, and other software relevant to the customer's use case. Lightsail instances are ideal for quick deployments to host simple web applications, websites, or business software. Lightsail instances are the quickest and easiest way for AWS developers to get started developing in the Cloud, and they are commonly used as environments for developing and testing applications. Lightsail offers templates to deploy instances with preconfigured operating systems, like Windows Server and Ubuntu Linux, preinstalled applications, like WordPress and Magento, and preloaded development stacks, like Node.js and LAMP. If a developer feels Lightsail is no longer ideal for their project or they want to move their application to a production environment, they can quickly and easily upgrade and migrate a Lightsail instance to an EC2 instance using the upgrade to EC2 wizard.

Continue learning about AWS Lightsail by browsing the AWS Lightsail web page at aws.amazon.com/lightsail/.

Define latency

Latency is one metric used to measure, predict, and define the performance of a system or solution. Latency is the time it takes to complete a given operation, such as a server reading data from a storage device. High latency often causes poor performance resulting in a bad user experience or reduced efficiency of the application or system. One common cause of high latency is geographic location. The further away a resource is from a user or application, the longer it will take for data and requests to move between them. AWS recommends launching resources in a Region close in proximity to users and applications to ensure low latency, optimized performance, and a positive user experience. If users are spread across the world, it may not be possible to launch resources close to all users. In those cases, AWS recommends using a content delivery network, like Amazon CloudFront, to distribute content to low latency Edge Locations across the world.

Continue learning about latency by browsing the What is Latency? web page at blog.stackpath.com/latency/.

Define throughput

Throughput is one metric used to measure, predict, and define the performance of a system or solution. Throughput is the amount of data that can be transferred to and from a device in a given period of time typically measured in multiples of bits per second (b/s or bps), such as Kb/s, Mb/s, and Gb/s. Throughput can also be measured in multiples of bytes per second (B/s or Bps), such as KB/s, MB/s, and GB/s. AWS uses multiples of bytes per second to measure and predict throughput of AWS resources. However, AWS doesn't use International System of Units (SI) metric prefixes to measure throughput many people are familiar with, such as kilo, mega, giga, and tera. Instead, AWS uses binary prefixes to measure throughput, such as kibi, mebi, gibi, and tebi. For example, instead of saying a Throughput Optimized HDD EBS volume is capable of 500 MB/s maximum throughput, AWS documentation will state a Throughput Optimized volume is capable of a maximum throughput of 500 MiB/s (pronounced mebibyte per second).

Continue learning about throughput by reading I/O size and volume throughput limits in the Storage, Amazon EBS, EBS performance, I/O characteristics and monitoring section of the Amazon Elastic Compute Cloud User Guide for Linux Instances.

Define IOPS

IOPS (Input/Output operations per second) is one metric used in storage performance optimization. IOPS alone is not typically used to measure the performance of a storage solution. Instead IOPS is used to predict and test how many read and write operations per second a storage solution can sustain over time before negatively impacting storage performance. The IOPS potential of a storage solution is dependent on a number of factors, including the size of I/O operations, the percentage of operations that are read and the percentage that are write, and whether the read and write operations are sequential or random.

Continue learning about IOPS by reading IOPS in the Storage, Amazon EBS, EBS performance, I/O characteristics and monitoring section of the Amazon Elastic Compute Cloud User Guide for Linux Instances.

Describe Amazon S3

Object storage, or object-based storage, is an unstructured data storage strategy in which data is stored and managed individually in distinct units called objects. An object includes the data file, any metadata that describes it, and a globally unique identifier. Amazon S3 (Simple Storage Service) is a cost-effective object storage service enabling customers to store massive amounts of data to be accessed by users and applications from anywhere. S3 is a highly reliable storage solution providing 99.999999999% (11 nines) durability and 99.99% availability of objects over a given year. This means that if a customer stores 10,000 objects with Amazon S3, they can expect to lose one object once every 10,000,000 years. With S3, customers create storage repositories called buckets to store data as objects within the AWS Region where they want the bucket and data within it to reside. After a bucket is created, customers upload objects to the bucket where they can be opened, downloaded or copied. When a bucket is first created, only the owner of the bucket can access the objects stored within it. However, customers can configure bucket policies, AWS IAM policies, access control lists (ACLs), and S3 Access Points to grant users and applications permission to access the bucket and control what they can do when accessing it. Customers commonly use S3 to host data for web applications, dynamic websites, and static websites. They also use S3 to store videos, music, photos, and software applications for users to download and as a target to backup data for disaster recovery and business continuity purposes. When uploading objects to a bucket, customers can choose between eight storage classes: S3 Standard, S3 Intelligent-Tiering, S3 Standard-IA, S3 One Zone-IA, S3 Glacier Instant Retrieval, S3 Glacier Flexible Retrieval, S3 Glacier Deep Archive, and S3 Outposts. The storage class selected depends on the customer's use case, how frequently the data will be accessed by users and applications, and how quickly the data must be accessible.

Continue learning about Amazon S3 by browsing the Amazon S3 web page at aws.amazon.com/s3/.

Describe the S3 Standard storage class

The Amazon S3 Standard storage class is designed for frequently accessed data and offers the highest performance of the S3 storage classes. S3 Standard is the best option for solutions in which data will be accessed often and there is a requirement for low latency, high throughput storage access. Common use cases for S3 Standard storage include cloud applications, dynamic websites, content distribution, gaming applications, and big data analytics.

Continue learning about the S3 Standard storage class by browsing the General Purpose section of the Object Storage Classes - Amazon S3 web page at aws.amazon.com/s3/storage-classes/#General_purpose/.

Describe the S3 Standard-IA storage class

The Amazon S3 Standard-IA storage class is designed for objects that are accessed less frequently than objects stored with S3 Standard but require the same performance in terms of access time, throughput, and latency. Objects stored with Standard-IA are available for millisecond access, similar to S3 Standard. Standard-IA provides a lower cost per GB of data stored compared to S3 Standard. However, AWS charges a retrieval fee for each object. Therefore, only objects that will be accessed infrequently should be stored with the storage class. The Standard-IA storage class is ideal for use cases in which cost can be optimized by sacrificing data availability, such as long-term storage, backups, and data stored for disaster recovery purposes.

Continue learning about the S3 Standard-IA storage class by browsing the Amazon S3 Standard-IA section of the Object Storage Classes - Amazon S3 web page at aws.amazon.com/s3/storage-classes/#Infrequent_access.

Describe the S3 One Zone-IA storage class

Objects stored with Amazon S3 storage classes are stored in a minimum of three Availability Zones for added resiliency with the exception of the One Zone-IA storage class. One Zone-IA is designed with the same performance capabilities of the Standard-IA storage class. However, since objects stored with One Zone-IA are stored in one Availability Zone, they cost 20% less on average than objects stored with Standard-IA. The One Zone-IA storage class is ideal for infrequently accessed data that can be re-created if the data is lost.

Continue learning about the S3 One Zone-IA storage class by browsing the Amazon S3 One Zone-IA section of the Object Storage Classes - Amazon S3 web page at aws.amazon.com/s3/storage-classes/#___.

Describe the S3 Glacier Instant Retrieval storage class

S3 Glacier storage classes are designed for low-cost data archiving. The S3 Glacier Instant Retrieval storage class is designed for data that is rarely accessed, approximately once per quarter, and requires millisecond access times. Objects stored with Glacier Instant Retrieval can be accessed with the same performance as objects stored with S3 Standard and Standard-IA in terms of access time, throughput, and latency. Glacier Instant Retrieval provides a low cost per GB of storage used and can save up to 68% compared to Standard-IA when archived objects are accessed once per quarter. However, AWS charges for retrieval of archived objects, and objects stored with Glacier Instant Retrieval incur the highest per retrieval cost. Therefore,

Instant Retrieval should only be used to store infrequently accessed data, such as medical images, new media assets, or user-generated content archival data.

Continue learning about the S3 Glacier Instant Retrieval storage class by browsing the Amazon S3 Glacier Instant Retrieval section of the Object Storage Classes - Amazon S3 web page at aws.amazon.com/s3/storage-classes/#Instant_Retrieval.

Describe the S3 Glacier Flexible Retrieval storage class

S3 Glacier storage classes are designed for low-cost data archiving. The S3 Glacier Flexible Retrieval storage class is designed for data that is rarely accessed, approximately once or twice per year, and may need to be retrieved within minutes. Objects stored with Glacier Flexible Retrieval are not available for real-time access. The objects must be retrieved, or restored, before they are accessible to users and applications. When objects are accessed once or twice per year, Glacier Flexible Retrieval can save up to 10% compared to Glacier Instant Retrieval. Objects in the Glacier Flexible Retrieval storage class have a minimum storage duration period of 90 days. If an object is deleted, overwritten, or transitioned to a different storage class before the 90-day minimum, AWS will charge the customer for 90 days of storage used. When objects are stored with Glacier Flexible Retrieval, they can be retrieved within 1-5 minutes with expedited retrieval incurring a per retrieval cost. Alternately, customers can request free bulk retrievals to make multiple objects available within 5-12 hours. Glacier Flexible Retrieval is ideal to store and retrieve large data sets without incurring retrieval cost, such as data backed up for disaster recovery purposes.

Continue learning about the S3 Glacier Flexible Retrieval storage class by browsing the Amazon S3 Glacier Flexible Retrieval section of the Object Storage Classes - Amazon S3 web page at aws.amazon.com/s3/storage-classes/#Flexible_Retrieval.

Describe the S3 Glacier Deep Archive storage class

S3 Glacier storage classes are designed for low-cost data archiving. S3 Glacier Deep Archive is the lowest cost storage class offered by Amazon S3 and is designed for preserving long-term data that is accessed once or twice per year. Objects stored with Glacier Deep Archive are not available for real-time access. The objects must be retrieved, or restored, before they are accessible to users and applications. Objects in the Glacier Deep Archive storage class have a minimum storage duration period of 180 days. If an object is deleted, overwritten, or transitioned to a different storage class before the 180-day minimum, AWS will charge the customer for 180 days of storage used. Objects stored with Glacier Deep Archive can be retrieved within 12 hours incurring a per retrieval cost. Alternately, customers can request free bulk retrievals to make multiple objects available within 48 hours. Glacier Deep Archive is a good alternative to magnetic tape systems and is ideal for customers in highly regulated industries in which data sets are often retained for 10 years or longer, such as financial services, healthcare, media and entertainment, and the public sector.

Continue learning about the S3 Glacier Deep Archive storage class by browsing the Amazon S3 Glacier Deep Archive section of the Object Storage Classes - Amazon S3 web page at aws.amazon.com/s3/storage-classes/#____.

Describe the S3 Intelligent-Tiering storage class

The Amazon S3 Intelligent-Tiering storage class is the only storage class that automatically optimizes storage costs by automatically moving objects between four access tiers based on how often the object is accessed. S3 Intelligent-Tiering includes two low latency, high performing tiers: Frequent Access and Infrequent Access. The other two tiers included are optional cost-effective archive tiers designed for access to objects that is not time sensitive: Archive Access and Deep Archive Access. When an object configured with the S3 Intelligent-Tiering storage class is uploaded to a bucket, the object is stored in the Frequent Access tier. If the object is not accessed for 30 consecutive days, it is moved to the Infrequent Access tier. If the Archive Access tier is activated and the object is not accessed for 90 consecutive days, it is moved to the Archive Access tier. If the Deep Archive Access tier is activated and the object is not accessed for 180 consecutive days, it is moved to the Deep Archive Access tier. When an object in the Infrequent Access tier is accessed, it is automatically moved back to the Frequent Access tier. If an object is moved to a Deep Archive tier, customers must manually restore a copy of the object before it can be accessed. The

S3 Intelligent-Tiering storage class is ideal for data with unknown or changing data access patterns.

Continue learning about the S3 Intelligent-Tiering storage class by browsing the S3 Intelligent-Tiering section of the Object Storage Classes - Amazon S3 web page at aws.amazon.com/s3/storage-classes/#Unknown_or_changing_access.

Describe S3 versioning

Versioning is a feature that can be enabled on an S3 bucket to store multiple versions of an object to ensure data can be recovered if an object is unintentionally overwritten or deleted. Enabling versioning only applies to new objects in a bucket. If versioning is enabled, S3 will not create versions of existing objects in the bucket. S3 retains all versions of an object in a bucket until they are manually or programmatically expired or permanently deleted. S3 Lifecycle configuration rules can be created and applied to an S3 bucket to automatically expire or permanently delete object versions.

Continue learning about S3 versioning by reading the Managing storage, Using S3 versioning section of the Amazon Simple Storage Service User Guide.

Describe an S3 Lifecycle configuration

An S3 Lifecycle configuration is a set of rules customers can apply to a group of objects to take two different types of actions: transition actions and expiration actions. Transition actions can be defined in configuration rules to transition objects to lower cost storage after a specified period of time. Transition actions can be used to move objects from Standard, Standard-IA, Intelligent-Tiering, and Glacier storage classes to any lower cost storage class. However, for the One Zone-IA storage class, transition actions can only be used to move objects to Glacier Flexible Retrieval or Deep Archive, not Glacier Instant Retrieval. Expiration actions can be defined in configuration rules to automatically delete objects from a bucket after a specified period of time.

Continue learning about S3 Lifecycle configuration rules by reading the Managing storage, Managing lifecycle section of the Amazon Simple Storage Service User Guide.

Describe S3 Object Lock

S3 Object Lock is a feature that can be enabled when creating an S3 bucket to store objects using a write-once-read-many, or WORM, model. Object Lock only works on buckets with versioning enabled. When Object Lock is enabled on an S3 bucket, the object versions stored in the bucket cannot be deleted or overwritten. S3 Object Lock is commonly used to prevent undesirable changes and deletion of object versions or to meet regulatory requirements that require WORM storage. When enabling Object Lock, customers can place a retention period on an object version to determine the period of time for which the version remains locked and cannot be deleted or overwritten. Customers can place a legal hold on an object version which locks the version indefinitely until the customer removes the legal hold.

Continue learning about S3 Object Lock by reading the Managing storage, Using Object Lock section of the Amazon Simple Storage Service User Guide.

Describe S3 replication

Replication is the automated process of copying objects to S3 buckets in the same AWS Region or in a different Region. Replication can be enabled on an S3 bucket by adding a replication rule to the bucket. Replication can be used for many purposes, including making copies of objects while retaining metadata, moving objects to a different storage class in partnership with lifecycle rules, copying data to a different bucket to change ownership, retaining replicas of objects in other Regions for disaster recovery purposes, or copying objects for access by users or applications in other Regions.

Continue learning about S3 replication by reading the Managing storage, Replicating objects section of the Amazon Simple Storage Service User Guide.

Describe Amazon S3 Transfer Acceleration

An Amazon S3 bucket is stored in an AWS Region a customer selects when creating the bucket. To reduce network latency and achieve optimal performance and user experience, it is recommended to create an S3 bucket in the same Region as the users, clients, and applications that will access objects in the bucket. Amazon S3 Transfer Acceleration is a feature that can be enabled on an S3 bucket to improve performance over long geographic locations and can be used when it is not possible to create a bucket in the same Region as the entities that will access it. Transfer Acceleration utilizes Amazon CloudFront edge locations distributed across the globe to route objects to and from an S3 bucket through an optimized network path. S3 Transfer Acceleration should be used for buckets that are located in a centralized location for global users, to more efficiently upload large amounts of data from on-premises environments to S3, or to transfer large amounts of data across continents.

Continue learning about Amazon S3 Transfer Acceleration by browsing the S3 Transfer Acceleration web page at aws.amazon.com/s3/transfer-acceleration/.

Describe S3 Batch Operations

There is no limit to the number of objects that can be stored in an S3 bucket. As a bucket grows, it can become difficult to manage each object in the bucket individually. In the past, customers relied on custom built applications that took months to develop to manage S3 objects. Amazon S3 Batch Operations is a data management feature enabling customers to manage billions of objects at scale using batch jobs. Customers can create batch jobs to perform management tasks on multiple objects simultaneously, such as configuring replication, replacing object tag sets, modifying access controls, restoring objects archived with S3 Glacier, and making changes to object properties.

Continue learning about S3 Batch Operations by browsing the Amazon S3 Batch Operations web page at aws.amazon.com/s3/features/batch-operations/.

Describe Amazon EBS

Block storage, or block level storage, is a structured data strategy in which storage systems break data into blocks and store each block in the most efficient place possible on the storage media. Block storage solutions are ideal for high throughput applications that perform long, continuous reads and writes, like streaming media apps, and transaction intensive applications that perform many random reads and writes, like database applications. Amazon Elastic Block Store (EBS) is a block storage service enabling customers to provision persistent storage volumes for use with Amazon EC2 instances. Customers can create an EBS volume and attach it to any instance that requires storage for data that is frequently accessed and updated. EBS volumes can only be attached to instances in the same Availability Zone (AZ), and by default, each volume can only be attached to one instance. However, customers can enable the EBS Multi-Attach feature on a volume and attach it to multiple EC2 instances in the same AZ. After a volume is attached to an instance, the volume acts as a virtual disk drive for the instance, and customers can use the volume as they would use any physical hard drive attached to a system. Any data stored in an EBS volume will be automatically replicated within the volume's AZ to prevent data loss in the case of a failure or disaster. EBS is an ideal storage solution for a wide range of use cases, such as relational and non-relational databases, enterprise applications, containerized applications, big data analytics engines, file systems, and streaming media.

Continue learning about Amazon EBS by browsing the Amazon Elastic Block Store web page at aws.amazon.com/ebs/.

Compare EBS SSD-backed and HDD-backed volumes

Amazon EBS offers different volume types to provide customers with options to balance performance and cost and tailor storage solutions to meet the specific needs of their systems and applications. EBS volume types fall into one of three categories: SSD-backed, HDD-backed, and previous generation. SSD-backed volumes have the highest cost and best performance in terms of IOPS potential and are ideal for workloads involving small frequent read and write operations, such as boot volumes and mission critical NoSQL and relational databases. HDD-backed volumes have lower cost and the best performance in terms of throughput and are ideal for workloads involving large streaming data sets, such as big data analytics and log processing. Previous generation volumes are available for backward compatibility. AWS does not recommend using previous generation volume types for new implementations.

Continue learning about EBS SSD-backed and HDD-backed volumes by browsing the Amazon EBS Volume Types web page at aws.amazon.com/ebs/volume-types/.

Describe EBS General Purpose volumes

Amazon EBS offers two categories of SSD-backed-volumes: General Purpose and Provisioned IOPS. General Purpose SSD volumes are recommended for most workloads and provide a balance of cost and performance. The General Purpose SSD volume types are gp3 and gp2. Both volume types support up to 3,000 IOPS for extended periods of time with the ability to burst to 16,000 IOPS based on a 1 TiB volume and an I/O size of 16 KiB. The primary differences between the General Purpose SSD volume types is the maximum supported throughput and price. EBS gp3 volumes support up to 1,000 MiB/s throughput per volume and cost $0.08 per GB of storage used per month, $0.005 per provisioned IOPS after 3,000 IOPS in a month, and $0.04 per provisioned MiB/s over 125 in a month. EBS gp2 volumes support up to 250 MiB/s and cost $0.10 per GB of storage used per month. General Purpose EBS volumes are ideal for boot volumes, dev/test environments, and applications that require low latency and high throughput at low cost, including Microsoft SQL Server databases, Cassandra databases, virtual desktops, and Hadoop analytics clusters.

Continue learning about EBS General Purpose volumes by browsing the Amazon EBS General Purpose Volumes web page at aws.amazon.com/ebs/general-purpose/.

Describe EBS Provisioned IOPS volumes

Amazon EBS offers two categories of SSD-backed-volumes: General Purpose and Provisioned IOPS. Provisioned IOPS SSD volumes are recommended for predictable mission critical applications requiring extremely low latency and high sustained IOPS performance. When creating a Provisioned IOPS volume, customers enter the maximum number of IOPS the volume should provide. The Provisioned IOPS volume types are io2 Block Express, io2, and io1. EBS io2 Block Express volumes are the highest performing and highest cost SSD-backed volumes capable of sub-millisecond latency and are designed for business-critical transactional workloads. Block Express volumes are capable of up to 256,000 IOPS and up to 4,000 Mib/s throughput per volume. Most EBS volumes can be a maximum of 16 TB in size. However, io2 Block Express volumes can be up to 64 TB in size. Most EBS volumes offer 99.9% durability (three nines availability). However, EBS io2 Block Express and io2 volumes offer greater availability with up to 99.999% durability (five nines availability). EBS io2 and io1 volumes are capable of up to 64,000 IOPS based on a 16 KiB I/O size and up to 4,000 MiB/s throughput per volume. EBS io2 Block Express and io2 volumes cost $0.125 per GB of storage used per month, $0.065 per provisioned IOPS per month up to 32,000 IOPS, $0.046 per provisioned IOPS per month from 32,001 to 64,000 IOPS, and $0.032 per provisioned IOPS per month for greater than 64,000 IOPS. EBS io1 volumes cost $0.125 per GB of storage used per month and $0.065 per provisioned IOPS per month. Provisioned IOPS volumes are ideal for mission-critical, I/O intensive NoSQL and relational databases.

Continue learning about EBS General Purpose volumes by browsing the Amazon EBS Provisioned IOPS Volume web page at aws.amazon.com/ebs/provisioned-iops/.

Describe EBS Throughput Optimized HDD volumes

Amazon EBS offers two categories of HDD-backed volumes: Throughput Optimized HDD and Cold HDD. Throughput Optimized HDD volumes are low cost and recommended for applications that require frequent data access, are not I/O intensive, and do not have strict latency requirements. EBS offers one Throughput Optimized HDD volume type, st1. EBS st1 volumes are capable of up to 500 MiB/s throughput and 500 IOPS based on 1 MiB I/O size and cost $0.045 per GB of storage used per month. Throughput Optimized HDD volumes are ideal for large, frequently accessed, throughput-intensive workloads such as Amazon EMR, ETL, data warehouses, and log processing.

Continue learning more about EBS Throughput Optimized HDD volumes by browsing the Amazon EBS Throughput Optimized HDD Volumes web page at aws.amazon.com/ebs/throughput-optimized/.

Describe EBS Cold HDD volumes

Amazon EBS offers two categories of HDD-backed volumes: Throughput Optimized HDD and Cold HDD. Cold HDD volumes are the lowest cost EBS volumes and are recommended for applications that require infrequent data access, are not I/O intensive, and do not have strict latency requirements. EBS offers one Cold HDD volume type, sc1. EBS sc1 volumes are capable of up to 250 MiB/s throughput and 250 IOPS based on 1 MiB I/O size and cost $0.015 per GB of storage used per month. Cold HDD volumes are ideal for large, sequential workloads that will rarely be accessed.

Continue learning more about EBS Cold HDD volumes by browsing the Amazon EBS Cold HDD Volumes web page at aws.amazon.com/ebs/cold-hdd/.

Describe Amazon EBS snapshots

Amazon EBS snapshots are incremental point-in-time copies of EBS volumes stored in S3 for long-term retention. Many storage administrators will say snapshots are not a backup. However, because EBS snapshots are not stored on the same physical storage as the original volume, they are considered incremental backups and can be used to restore an EBS volume to a point-in-time and recover data in the case of a disaster or failure. EBS snapshots can be created manually by customers, they can be created programmatically, or they can be created automatically using Amazon Data Lifecycle Manager. Data Lifecycle Manager (DLM) is a feature for EBS snapshots that simplifies automatically backing up EBS volumes by enabling customers to create and delete snapshots based on a custom schedule. When a volume is created from a snapshot, the volume is an exact replica of the original volume at the exact time the snapshot was created. EBS snapshots are commonly used for disaster recovery purposes, to migrate data across Regions, accounts, and Availability Zones, and to comply with backup standards and regulations.

Continue learning about Amazon EBS snapshots by browsing the Amazon EBS Snapshots web page at aws.amazon.com/ebs/snapshots/.

Describe Amazon EFS

File storage, or file level storage, is an unstructured data strategy in which data is stored as files in a file system providing shared access to users, applications, and other resources. Amazon EFS (Elastic File Storage) is a file storage service designed to provide shared access to files using the NFS protocol to Amazon EC2 instances, ECS containers, AWS Lambda functions, and on-premises servers. Customers can create an EFS file system using the EC2 Launch Instance Wizard, EFS console, CLI, or API. Then, they can mount the file system on thousands of compute resources allowing simultaneous access to files in the file system. As files are added to a file system, EFS automatically grows storage and throughput capacity with no need for management or provisioning by the customer. As files are removed, EFS automatically shrinks capacity. EFS automatically stores file system data in multiple Availability Zones (AZs) for Standard storage classes and redundantly within a single AZ for One Zone storage classes. EFS is an optimal storage solution for machine learning and big data analytics workloads, content management systems, user home directories, and services and applications that require simultaneous access to a storage resource.

Continue learning about Amazon EFS by browsing Amazon EFS web page at aws.amazon.com/efs/.

Compare Amazon EFS performance modes

Amazon EFS offers two performance modes that can be configured when a file system is created but cannot be changed on existing file systems: General Purpose and Max I/O. The General Purpose performance mode is the default mode and recommended for the majority of EFS workloads that are sensitive to latency, such as web servers, content management systems, and user home directories. The Max I/O performance mode is recommended for workloads that have high throughput and

IOPS requirements, such as big data analytics, media processing, and genomics analysis.

Continue learning about Amazon EFS performance modes by reading Performance modes in the Performance section of the Amazon Elastic File System User Guide.

Compare Amazon EFS throughput modes

Amazon EFS offers two throughput modes that can be configured when a file system is created and can be changed on existing file systems: Bursting Throughput and Provisioned Throughput. With Bursting Throughput mode, the amount of throughput available depends on the size of the file system due to the distributed nature of the Amazon EFS infrastructure. Larger file systems provide greater throughput, and smaller file systems provide less throughput. File Systems in Bursting Throughput mode accumulate credits when throughput is below a baseline rate based on the size of the file system. When throughput requirements for a file system burst above the baseline rate, the file system uses accrued credits to service the clients that require additional throughput. Burstable Throughput mode is ideal for most file system-based workloads. With Provisioned Throughput mode, an AWS consumer can set the throughput limit regardless of the size of the file system. Provisioned Throughput mode is ideal for workloads with predictable throughput requirements and for use cases where the client or application requires high throughput to access a small amount of data.

Continue learning about Amazon EFS throughput modes by reading Throughput modes in the Performance section of the Amazon Elastic File System User Guide.

Describe EFS lifecycle management

EFS lifecycle management is a feature that can be configured on an EFS file system to optimize storage cost. When lifecycle management is configured, files that are not access in a given period of time are automatically moved from the higher priced EFS Standard storage class to the lower priced Infrequent Access storage class. When configuring lifecycle management, customers can configure the lifecycle policy to move files if they haven't been accessed in either 7, 14, 30, 60, or 90 days.

Continue learning about EFS lifecycle management by reading the Managing file systems, EFS lifecycle management section of the Amazon Elastic File System User Guide.

Describe EFS replication

EFS replication is a feature enabling customers to create a replica, or copy, of their EFS file system in an AWS Region of their choice. When replication is enabled on a file system, EFS automatically replicates files and metadata in the source file system to the destination file system with no impact on performance to the source. Replication is commonly used for disaster recovery purposes and to meet any compliance requirements customers must adhere to by storing copies of data in multiple geographic locations separated by a certain distance.

Continue learning about EFS replication by browsing the Data protection section of the Amazon Elastic File System (EFS) Features web page at aws.amazon.com/efs/features/#Data_protection.

Describe AWS Storage Gateway

AWS Storage Gateway is a hybrid cloud storage service enabling customers to provide their on-premises applications, services, and users access to their AWS Cloud storage resources. With Storage Gateway customers set up a gateway device, connect it to AWS, configure the storage resources to be shared between AWS and on-premises environments, and connect the storage resources to the on-premises clients that require access to the data in the AWS Cloud. After configuring the gateway and storage resources, on-premises applications, services, and users will be able to access the data for their use case. Customers commonly use Storage Gateway to backup or migrate data to the Cloud, present file shares from the Cloud to on-premises users, and provide on-premises applications low latency access to data stored in their AWS environment. When planning for and setting up a gateway device, customers have three options to host the gateway. Customers can host their gateway on an EC2 instance in the AWS Cloud, on an on-premises virtual machine running on VMware ESXi, Microsoft Hyper-V, or Linux KVM, or on a dedicated hardware appliance they purchase from AWS and install in their data center.

Continue learning about AWS Storage Gateway by browsing the AWS Storage Gateway web page at aws.amazon.com/storagegateway/.

Describe AWS Backup

AWS Backup is a service enabling centralized and automated backup of AWS resources, such as EBS volumes, EC2 instances, and RDS databases, across multiple AWS accounts and Regions. Many AWS services have backup functionality and features built-in. However, centrally managing the backup of all resources with AWS Backup provides simplicity and ensures data across all resources in a solution are backed up and protected. With AWS Backup, customers create policy-based backup plans including a schedule with backup start times, frequency, and backup window. Backup plans include backup retention policies to remove backups that are no longer needed as well as lifecycle management policies that will automatically transition backups from warm storage to cold storage to ensure compliance requirements are met while minimizing storage costs.

Continue learning about AWS Backup by browsing the AWS Backup web page at aws.amazon.com/backup/.

Describe AWS Snowball

AWS Snowball is a data migration, edge computing, and edge storage device enabling customers to securely transfer large amounts of data into and out of the AWS Cloud without incurring high Internet charges. Snowball is the mid-sized member of the Snow Family and is capable of petabyte-scale data transfer. Snowball offers two different types of devices, Snowball devices and Snowball Edge devices. Snowball devices are simply used for migrating data between customers' on-premises data storage and Amazon S3 storage. Snowball Edge devices have built-in compute capabilities and are used by customers to perform edge computing and storage tasks on-premises, like analyzing data to gain insights, prior to migrating the data to Amazon S3 storage. When a customer needs to import data from on-premises storage to the AWS Cloud or export data from the Cloud to on-prem storage, they create a job in the AWS Snow Family Management Console or through the job management API. If the customer is exporting data from AWS to on-premises, AWS exports the data onto the Snowball device and ships it to the customer. Then, the customer transfers the data from the device to their on-premises storage resources and ships the device back to AWS. If the customer is importing data from on-premises to AWS, AWS ships the Snowball device to the customer, the customer transfers data from their on-premises storage resources to the device, and they ship the device back to AWS. When AWS receives the device, they import the data to the AWS Cloud.

Continue learning about AWS Snowball by browsing the AWS Snowball web page at aws.amazon.com/snowball/.

Describe AWS Snowcone

AWS Snowcone is a data migration, edge computing, and edge storage device enabling customers to securely transfer terabytes of data into and out of the AWS Cloud without incurring high Internet charges. AWS Snowcone is the smallest member of the Snow Family. Snowcone offers an HDD version equipped with 8 terabytes (TB) of usable storage and an SSD version equipped with 14 TB of usable storage. Snowcone offers two different types of devices, Snowcone devices and Snowcone Edge devices. Snowcone devices are simply used for migrating data between customers' on-premises data storage and Amazon S3 storage. Snowcone Edge devices have built-in compute capabilities and are used by customers to perform edge computing and storage tasks on-premises, like analyzing data to gain insights, prior to migrating the data to Amazon S3 storage. When a customer needs to import data from on-premises storage to the AWS Cloud or export data from the Cloud to on-prem storage, they create a job in the AWS Snow Family Management Console or through the job management API. If the customer is exporting data from AWS to on-premises, AWS exports the data onto the Snowcone device and ships it to the customer. Then, the customer transfers the data from the device to their on-premises storage resources and ships the device back to AWS. If the customer is importing data from on-premises to AWS, AWS ships the Snowcone device to the customer, the customer transfers data from their on-premises storage resources to the device, and they ship the device back to AWS. When AWS receives the device, they import the data to the AWS Cloud.

Continue learning about AWS Snowcone by browsing the AWS Snowcone web page at aws.amazon.com/snowcone/.

Describe AWS Snowmobile

The largest member of the Snow Family, AWS Snowmobile, is a fully managed service enabling exabyte-scale data transfer from on-premises environments to the AWS Cloud. Each Snowmobile device is stored in a 45-foot-long ruggedized shipping container pulled by a semi-trailer truck and is capable of transferring up to 100 petabytes (PB) of data. When customers have many PB or exabytes (EB) of data to transfer to their AWS environment, AWS personnel first perform an initial assessment of the customer's environment and data. Then, one or more Snowmobile devices are transported to the customer's data center. When the Snowmobile arrives on site, AWS personnel will work with the customer's team to connect high-speed networking devices from the Snowmobile to their local network. Then, the customer will begin transferring data to the Snowmobile. When the data transfer is complete, the Snowmobile will be driven back to AWS, and AWS personnel will import the data into Amazon S3.

Continue learning about AWS Snowmobile by browsing the AWS Snowmobile web page at aws.amazon.com/snowmobile/.

Describe Amazon DynamoDB

Amazon DynamoDB is a fully managed key-value NoSQL database service providing customers with high performing databases without the need to provision, patch, and manage servers. With DynamoDB data is stored as items in a table, and each item has attributes associated to identify and define the item. An example of how data is stored in DynamoDB is a table named Users that stores data about each employee in a company. In the Users table there will be an item for each employee, and each item will have the attributes of the employee, such as a Name attribute of John Smith and a Title attribute of Systems Administrator. DynamoDB tables are automatically replicated to multiple Availability Zones (AZ) to ensure the data is always available should a failure or disaster occur in an AZ. DynamoDB tables are automatically scaled up and down to adjust capacity and maintain performance for applications. DynamoDB is ideal to store data for applications that require a predictable, high performing database at a low cost, such as web applications, mobile backends, and microservices.

Continue learning about Amazon DynamoDB by browsing the Amazon DynamoDB web page at aws.amazon.com/dynamodb/.

Describe DynamoDB Accelerator

Amazon DynamoDB Accelerator (DAX) is a feature of DynamoDB providing managed in-memory cache to deliver microsecond latency while servicing millions of requests from applications running on EC2 instances in a VPC. DAX is deployed as a cluster in the same VPC as the EC2 instances that will host the applications utilizing the cluster for in-memory cache. Applications that utilize the cluster are deployed on the EC2 instances using the DAX client. DAX is optimal for applications that require sub-millisecond latency, perform frequent small read operations, and request the same data from large data sets. DAX is not optimal for applications that require consistent reads or perform frequent write operations.

Continue learning more about DynamoDB Accelerator by browsing the Amazon DynamoDB Accelerator (DAX) web page at aws.amazon.com/dynamodb/dax/.

Describe DynamoDB global tables

DynamoDB global tables is a performance feature of DynamoDB enabling customers to deploy fully managed, multi-region, and multi-active databases for massively scaled, global applications. A global table is a collection of identical DynamoDB tables in one or more AWS Region all owned by a single AWS account. A replica table is a single table that functions as a part of a global table. When customers create a global table, they create a replica table in each Region where their global application will run. When the application writes data to a replica table, DynamoDB automatically replicates the changes to all other replica tables in the global table to ensure all replica tables are identical. Without the global tables feature, customers would need to create a custom replication solution to maintain continuity across tables in a database solution for global applications. DynamoDB global tables enable customers to deliver low-latency database access to their users and deliver optimized performance for massively scaled applications with globally dispersed users.

Continue learning about DynamoDB tables by browsing the Amazon DynamoDB global tables web page at aws.amazon.com/dynamodb/global-tables/.

Describe DynamoDB point-in-time recovery

DynamoDB point-in-time recovery (PITR) is an availability feature of DynamoDB enabling customers to protect their tables from accidental write and delete operations. When customers enable PITR on a table, DynamoDB automatically creates continuous backups of the table every second. Each backup is kept for 35 days ensuring customers can restore the table to any second within the past 35 days. DynamoDB continues to create backups of the table until the customer disables PITR on the table. DynamoDB PITR ensures customers never have to worry about creating, maintaining, or scheduling on-demand backups of their DynamoDB tables.

Continue learning about DynamoDB point-in-time recovery by browsing the Point-in-time recovery (PITR) for Amazon DynamoDB web page at aws.amazon.com/dynamodb/pitr/.

Describe Amazon RDS

Amazon RDS (Relational Database Service) is a fully managed database service enabling customers to deploy relational databases without the need to provision, patch, license, and manage servers. RDS automates common administration tasks, like software patching, licensing, hardware provisioning, database setup, and backups, enabling customers to focus more time on developing their applications and less time on maintaining their databases. When a customer creates a database (DB) instance, they select the instance class type, which determines the CPU and memory capacity available for the instance. The customer also selects the storage type, which determines the storage performance they can expect. RDS DB instances include an EC2 instance for compute and an EBS volume for storage resources. However, the EC2 instance and EBS volume are fully managed by RDS. With RDS, a customer can create a DB instance with a PostgreSQL, MySQL, MariaDB, Oracle, Microsoft SQL Server, or Amazon Aurora database engine. As the customer's database needs change, they can quickly scale the DB instance up or down by changing the instance class type to add more compute and memory capacity or by adding more storage capacity to the database. Amazon Aurora databases automatically scale storage capacity up and down to meet demand. However, other database engines supported with RDS require a customer to manually add or remove storage capacity. By default, RDS automatically backs up DB instances to Amazon S3 based on a customer defined retention period and backup window ensuring customers can restore their databases to a point in time should a failure or disaster occur that results in data loss. RDS is ideal to store data for applications that require assured data integrity and reliability, such as ecommerce applications and mission critical enterprise applications.

Continue learning about Amazon RDS by browsing the Amazon RDS web page at aws.amazon.com/rds/.

Describe RDS Multi-AZ deployments

RDS Multi-AZ is an availability feature of Amazon RDS enabling customers to deploy a primary DB instance and standby instances in up to three different Availability Zones (AZs). Multi-AZ deployments provide high availability and failover support for RDS DB instances. With Multi-AZ deployments, customers can deploy either one or two standby instances in different AZs. When customers deploy one standby instance, it is called a Multi-AZ DB instance deployment. When customers deploy two standby instances, it is called a Multi-AZ DB cluster deployment. The standby instance in a Multi-AZ DB instance deployment only provides failover support and cannot serve any database traffic. However, the standby instances in a Multi-AZ DB cluster provide failover support and can also serve read requests from applications. Customers can deploy a Multi-AZ instance or cluster when creating a new DB instance, or they can modify an existing instance to convert the instance to a Multi-AZ deployment. When a Multi-AZ instance or cluster is deployed, RDS automatically replicates any changes from the primary DB instance to the standby instances. If a planned or unplanned outage occurs with the primary instance, RDS automatically fails over to a standby instance in another AZ. Multi-AZ deployments are available for all RDS supported database engines, including Amazon Aurora, MySQL, PostgreSQL, Oracle, and SQL Server.

Continue learning about RDS Multi-AZ deployments by browsing the Amazon RDS Multi-AZ Deployments web page at aws.amazon.com/rds/features/multi-az/.

Describe RDS database snapshots

RDS DB instances are automatically backed up daily. However, customers can create manual backups of their instance at any point in time by creating a database (DB) snapshot. An RDS DB snapshot is a point-in-time copy of the entire DB instance, not just individual databases. Customers can create a new DB instance or restore a DB instance to a point in time by restoring from a DB snapshot. Customers can create DB snapshots and perform other management tasks using the AWS Management Console, CLI, or the RDS API. DB snapshots can only be restored to the same AWS Region where they were created. To restore a snapshot to another Region, customers can copy the snapshot to the other Region and quickly deploy a copy of the DB instance in the Region. RDS manual snapshots can be shared between different AWS accounts. However, RDS automated snapshots cannot be shared with other AWS accounts. To share automated snapshots, customers must first copy the snapshot to make a manual version. Another key difference between automated and manual snapshots is automated snapshots expire between 0 and 35 days from creation, but manual snapshots never expire. When a manual snapshot is no longer needed, customers must manually delete the snapshot.

Continue learning about RDS database snapshots by reading the Backing up and restoring a DB instance, Creating a DB snapshot section of the Amazon Relational Database Service User Guide.

Describe RDS read replicas

Customers can create an RDS read replica of their DB instance to reduce the load on their databases. When creating a read replica, customers first specify an existing DB instance as the source. Then, RDS takes a snapshot of the DB instance and creates a read-only instance from the snapshot. Whenever changes are made to the source instance, RDS replicates the changes to the read replica. Read replicas can be created in the same Region as the source DB instance or in another Region to improve performance of read queries from applications in the Region. Customers can connect their applications to the read replica just like they would any other database. The only difference is the read replica is read-only, so the applications will only be able to read from the database and not write to it. In addition to reducing the load on the source database, read replicas can be used to continue serving read requests when the source database is unavailable, to support business reporting queries and data warehousing scenarios, and as a disaster recovery solution in which customers can promote a read replica to a standalone instance if the source database experiences a failure.

Continue learning about RDS read replicas by browsing the Amazon RDS Read Replicas web page at aws.amazon.com/rds/features/read-replicas/.

Describe Amazon Aurora

Amazon Aurora is a fully managed database service enabling customers to create databases compatible with MySQL or PostgreSQL database engines without the need to provision, patch, and manage servers. Aurora instances are managed by Amazon RDS, and customers can create an Aurora database instance in the Amazon RDS Management Console. Aurora enables high availability and fault tolerance by automatically replicating the data in a database instance to multiple Availability Zones, by backing up the data to Amazon S3, and by automatically scaling storage capacity for database instances to meet demand. Aurora provides better performance than traditional relational database services due to its architecture and by allowing customers to create read replicas of a database instance in Regions closest to clients and users of the database ensuring low-latency to those who most often access the data. Aurora is ideal to store data for applications that require both consistent performance and reliability, such as mission critical enterprise applications, SaaS applications, and web and mobile gaming.

Continue learning about Amazon Aurora by browsing the Amazon Aurora web page at aws.amazon.com/rds/aurora/.

Describe Amazon Redshift

Amazon Redshift is a data warehouse service enabling customers to store structured and semi-structured data from multiple sources and analyze the data to gain insight into their business and customers. With Redshift, customers create a cluster of databases and load their data to the databases in the cluster. Once data is loaded to the cluster, customers can analyze the data by querying the databases using the query editor in the Redshift console or by connecting any external SQL client tool to the cluster. With Redshift, customers can also query data from outside sources by using Redshift Spectrum to query data in Amazon S3, by sharing data between Redshift clusters, or by joining data from an RDS database, Aurora database, or S3 bucket with the data stored in Redshift clusters. Redshift machine learning (Redshift ML) is a predictive analytics feature enabling customers to predict future outcomes by integrating Redshift data warehousing with the Amazon SageMaker machine learning service to create, train, and deploy machine learning models. Redshift is commonly used to improve financial and demand forecasts, collaborate and share data, optimize business intelligence, and increase developer productivity.

Continue learning about Amazon Redshift by browsing the Amazon Redshift web page at aws.amazon.com/redshift/.

Describe Amazon ElastiCache

In-memory databases store data in running memory instead of persistent storage to provide sub-millisecond latency for I/O operations and deliver ultra-fast application performance. Amazon ElastiCache is a service that offers in-memory databases that sit between an application and the application's data store, such as an RDS DB instance. Elasticache functions as a buffer or cache to store ultrafast read copies of data enabling customers to deliver microsecond read latency to their applications that require real-time data access. ElastiCache offers two in-memory database engines: ElastiCache for Redis and ElastiCache for Memcached. Memcached is ideal for providing session storage to clients and for use cases in which a simple data caching model and the ability to scale as demand changes are important. Specific use cases for ElastiCache for Memcached include web, mobile, gaming, ad-tech, and e-commerce applications. Redis is ideal for use cases in which caching complex data types, connecting to multiple databases, sorting and ranking in-memory datasets, security & compliance, and high availability & fault tolerance are important. Specific use cases for ElastiCache for Redis include gaming leaderboards, geospatial applications, ad targeting, social media analytics, chat and messaging, and media streaming.

Continue learning about Amazon ElastiCache by browsing the Amazon ElastiCache web page at aws.amazon.com/elasticache/.

Describe Amazon VPC

Amazon VPC (Virtual Private Cloud) is a networking service enabling customers to isolate traffic between their AWS resources with a virtual network called a virtual private cloud (VPC). An AWS resource, such as an EC2 instance, must be launched in a VPC when the resource is created. If a customer does not specify which VPC to launch the resource in, it is launched in the default VPC that is automatically generated with every AWS account. Customers can create, access, and manage VPCs using the VPC console in the AWS Management Console or using the AWS CLI, SDKs, or API. In the VPC console, customers can create a VPC using the VPC Wizard to choose one of four configurations: VPC with a single public subnet, VPC with public and private subnets (NAT), VPC with public and private subnets and AWS Site-to-Site VPN access, or VPC with a private subnet only and AWS Site-to-Site VPN access. After the VPC is created with one of the configurations, customers can customize the VPC to fit their needs more closely by creating subnets, internet or NAT gateways, route tables, network ACLs, and other VPC networking features.

Continue learning about Amazon VPC by browsing the Amazon Virtual Private Cloud web page at aws.amazon.com/vpc/.

Describe a VPC subnet

Every device on a network must have an IP address. The IP address helps ensure data and requests are sent to the correct device. A subnet is a way of dividing a larger network into smaller networks to ensure data and requests take the most efficient and fastest path to a device on a network. Each subnet has a range of IP addresses that can be assigned to devices in the subnet. When an administrator wants to add a device to the subnet, they simply assign an IP address to the device that is within the range of IP addresses in the subnet. AWS customers can create multiple subnets in a VPC to segment the VPC into smaller networks and improve security, performance, and network efficiency. Each subnet created can only span one Availability Zone. When customers create a VPC, they configure a range of IPv4 addresses for the VPC in CIDR notation. This is the primary CIDR block of IP addresses that can be assigned to devices in the VPC. When customers create a subnet in a VPC, they must configure an IPv4 CIDR block from the primary CIDR block to assign IP addresses to resources in the subnet. Customers can also configure an Availability Zone (AZ) for a subnet to ensure resources launched in the subnet reside in a specific AZ. If no AZ is specified when a subnet is created, AWS will choose an AZ for the subnet.

Continue learning about VPC subnets by reading the Subnets section of the Amazon Virtual Private Cloud User Guide.

Describe a VPC route table

A VPC route table is a set of rules, called routes, which tell subnets and gateways in a VPC where network traffic should be directed, or routed. When a VPC is created, a main route table is automatically created for the VPC. Customers can create custom route tables to keep the main route table intact and associate any subnets they create with a custom route table to explicitly control how each subnet routes traffic. Each subnet in a VPC must be associated with only one route table. If customers do not explicitly associate a subnet to a route table when they create it, the subnet will be automatically associated with the VPC's main route table.

Continue learning about VPC route tables by reading the Subnets, Route tables section of the Amazon Virtual Private Cloud User Guide.

Describe an internet gateway

By default, compute resources in a subnet cannot communicate with the Internet. An internet gateway is a virtual device that can be created and attached to a VPC to enable bidirectional communication between compute resources residing in public subnets and the Internet. Each VPC can only have one attached internet gateway, and each internet gateway can only be attached to one VPC. When customers attach an internet gateway to a VPC, they also need to add a route to the route table associated with the subnet that requires access to the Internet. The route should be created with the subnet configured as the Destination and the internet gateway configured as the Target. To configure Internet access for all subnets associated with the route table, a route can be created with 0.0.0.0/0 configured as the Destination and the internet gateway configured as the Target.

Continue learning about internet gateways by reading the Connect your VPC, Internet gateways section of the Amazon Virtual Private Cloud User Guide.

Describe a NAT gateway

A NAT gateway is a virtual device that can be created in a VPC to enable compute resources in a private subnet to communicate with the Internet. A NAT gateway allows outbound traffic from the compute resources in the private subnet to the Internet but does not allow inbound traffic from the Internet to the resources. A NAT gateway enables compute resources to use the Internet for common maintenance tasks, such as applying patches or downloading new software packages while keeping the resources safe from potential external attacks launched over the Internet. A NAT gateway requires Internet connectivity, so it should be created in a public subnet in the VPC. Then, a route needs to be added to the route table the private subnet is associated with, and the NAT gateway should be configured as the Destination and the internet gateway should be configured as the Target. When customers create a NAT gateway, they must attach an elastic IP address to the NAT gateway. Therefore, an available elastic IP address must be provisioned to the AWS account and cannot be attached to any compute resource or network interface. An elastic IP address is a static IPv4 address that is allocated to an AWS account and can be associated with an instance or network interface in any VPC. An elastic IP is free while it is associated with a running instance or attached network interface but is billed a small hourly charge when unassociated, associated with a stopped instance, or associated with an unattached interface.

Continue learning about NAT gateways by reading the Connect your VPC, NAT devices, NAT gateways section of the Amazon Virtual Private Cloud User Guide.

Compare public and private subnets

A public subnet is a subnet that has a route to an internet gateway enabling connectivity from the compute resources in the public subnet outbound to the Internet and from the Internet inbound to the resources. A private subnet is a subnet that has no route to an internet gateway ensuring no inbound traffic from the internet can reach the compute resources in the subnet. Private subnets can only access the Internet outbound if a NAT gateway is created in a public subnet and a route from the NAT gateway to an internet gateway is created in the route table associated with the private subnet.

Continue learning about public and private subnets by reading Public and private subnets in the Scenarios, VPC with public and private subnets (NAT) section of the Amazon Virtual Private Cloud User Guide.

Describe VPC peering

By default, AWS resources in separate VPCs cannot communicate with each other. A VPC peering connection is a networking connection that can be configured to connect two VPCs together and enable resources in each VPC to communicate with each other using private IP addresses without the use of a gateway or VPN connection. VPC peering enables resources in separate VPCs to communicate with each other as if they were on the same network. VPC peering connections can be created to connect VPCs in the same AWS account or different accounts and can also be created to connect VPCs in different AWS Regions. VPC peering connections cannot be created between VPC's with overlapping IP CIDR blocks or between VPCs if one of the following connectivity options is already configured for either VPC, a VPN, Direct Connect, an internet gateway, a NAT device, or ClassicLink.

Continue learning about VPC peering by reading the What is VPC peering? Section of the Amazon Virtual Private Cloud User Guide.

Describe VPC endpoints

By default, AWS resources in a VPC can only communicate with other resources in the same VPC. In order for resources within a VPC to communicate with other resources, AWS offers a variety of virtual devices and connectivity options customers can implement in their AWS environment. A VPC endpoint is a virtual device that enables AWS resources in a VPC to communicate with resources outside of the VPC within the same Region using the AWS network instead of the Internet. By ensuring traffic does not traverse the Internet, VPC endpoints help provide low network latency and more predictable network performance. When a VPC endpoint is created, the

AWS customer must associate the endpoint with one or more subnets and the AWS service, such as Amazon S3, in which the resources to be accessed are hosted. After the VPC endpoint is created and configured, the endpoint allows resources in the associated subnets to access resources hosted with the associated AWS service. AWS offers three different types of VPC endpoints: Gateway Load Balancer endpoints for accessing targets registered with a Gateway Load Balancer, gateway endpoints for accessing resources hosted with Amazon S3 or DynamoDB, and interface endpoints for accessing resources hosted with other AWS services.

Continue learning about VPC endpoints by reading VPC endpoints in the Concepts section of the Amazon Virtual Private Cloud User Guide for AWS PrivateLink.

Describe Elastic Load Balancing

Elastic Load Balancing (ELB) is a networking service enabling customers to automatically distribute incoming traffic amongst multiple compute resources, such as EC2 instances, ECS containers, and Lambda functions. When a customer wants to spread traffic across compute resources, they create a load balancer using the AWS Management Console, CLI, SDKs, or API. Once the load balancer is created, the customer adds targets, such as EC2 instances, to the load balancer to begin distributing traffic to the targets. Elastic Load Balancing optimizes performance by ensuring the load is balanced evenly across targets and no resource is overloaded with traffic and improves scalability by enabling customers to remove or add targets to a load balancer with no disruption in service. Elastic Load Balancing also ensures resiliency and availability by monitoring the health of targets added to the load balancer and halting traffic to unhealthy targets until the resource is once again healthy or manually replaced. Elastic Load Balancing is commonly used as a decoupling mechanism to modernize applications with multi-tier architectures and microservices and to improve hybrid cloud network scalability by balancing load across AWS and on-premises resources. Customers can choose between four types of load balancer offered by AWS depending on their use case: Application Load Balancer, Network Load Balancer, Gateway Load Balancer, and Classic Load Balancer. AWS offers Classic Load Balancers for backward compatibility with environments utilizing EC2-Classic. For all new load balancing implementations, AWS recommends choosing an Application, Network, or Gateway Load Balancer depending on the use case.

Continue learning about Elastic Load Balancing by browsing the Elastic Load Balancing web page at aws.amazon.com/elasticloadbalancing/.

Understand when to use a Network Load Balancer

The type of load balancer customers choose with Elastic Load Balancing depends on the needs of their applications. Customers should choose a Network Load Balancer (NLB) if their applications require extreme performance or a static IP address. A Network Load Balancer serves as a single point of contact for clients and distributes traffic across multiple supported targets hosting application components. The targets supported by Network Load Balancers include IP addresses, EC2 instances, containers, and Application Load Balancers. Network Load Balancers can be configured to listen for requests and route them to target groups using TCP, UDP, and TLS protocols. A Network Load Balancer determines which target to send a request to using a flow hash algorithm based on the protocol, the source IP and port, and the destination IP and port.

Continue learning about Network Load Balancers by browsing the Network Load Balancer web page at aws.amazon.com/elasticloadbalancing/network-load-balancer/.

Understand when to use an Application Load Balancer

The type of load balancer customers choose with Elastic Load Balancing depends on the needs of their applications. Application Load Balancers (ALB) are specifically designed for HTTP & HTTPS web applications. Customers should choose an ALB if their applications require flexibility of management or the use of Lambda functions. An Application Load Balancer serves as a single point of contact for clients and distributes application traffic across multiple supported targets hosting application components. The targets supported by Application Load Balancers include IP addresses, EC2 instances, containers, and Lambda functions. Application Load Balancers can be configured to listen for requests from clients and route them to target groups using HTTP, HTTPS, and gRPC protocols. An Application Load Balancer determines which target to send a request to based on a user configured routing algorithm, round robin or least outstanding requests.

Continue learning about Application Load Balancers by browsing the Application Load Balancer web page at aws.amazon.com/elasticloadbalancing/application-load-balancer/.

Understand when to use a Gateway Load Balancer

The type of load balancer customers choose with Elastic Load Balancing depends on the needs of their applications. Customers should choose a Gateway Load Balancer (GWLB) if they are using a fleet of 3rd party virtual security appliances running on EC2 instances to inspect application traffic for potential security issues. Common 3rd party virtual security appliances include firewalls, intrusion prevention systems, and deep packet inspection systems. When a Gateway Load Balancer receives application traffic, it forwards the traffic to a healthy and available virtual security appliance that is registered with the load balancer as a target. The virtual appliance then inspects the traffic and either drops the traffic if the appliance finds a potential security issue or forwards the traffic back to the Gateway Load Balancer if the traffic is deemed safe. If the Gateway Load Balancer receives the application traffic back from the virtual appliance, it forwards the traffic to the destination. If the destination sends a response back to the source, the traffic follows the same path through the Gateway Load Balancer and the same virtual appliance before it is forwarded back to the source.

Continue learning about Gateway Load Balancers by browsing the Gateway Load Balancer web page at aws.amazon.com/elasticloadbalancing/gateway-load-balancer/.

Describe Amazon CloudFront

A content delivery network (CDN) is a network of servers distributed across geographic locations capable of sharing web content, such as images and videos, with each other and delivering the content to websites, applications, and end users.

The goal of a CDN is to place content on the servers closest to the sites, apps, and users that will access the content to optimize performance, ensure availability, and improve user experience. Amazon CloudFront is a content delivery network service enabling customers to deliver static and dynamic web content, such as .html, .css, .php, image, video, and audio files, to their websites, applications, and end users globally. CloudFront optimizes the reliability, performance, and security of content delivered to websites and applications. To get started delivering content with CloudFront, a customer creates a CloudFront distribution and selects the origin, such as an S3 bucket or web server, that stores the content for their website or application. When an end user accesses the website or application, CloudFront delivers the content to a CloudFront Edge Location closest to the end user. By default, content is stored in the Edge Location for 24 hours to ensure optimized performance and user experience while the end user accesses the content through the website or application.

Continue learning about Amazon CloudFront by browsing the Amazon CloudFront web page at aws.amazon.com/cloudfront/.

Describe CloudFront for Media & Entertainment use cases

Amazon CloudFront is optimized for Media & Entertainment industry workloads and is highly capable of distributing streaming video to viewers across the world. Two common Media & Entertainment use cases for CloudFront are streaming video-on-demand (VOD) and live video streaming. Customers can deliver large catalogs of VOD content to global viewers using Amazon S3 to store the video in its original format, a video encoder, like AWS Elemental Media Convert, to transcode the video into streaming formats, and CloudFront to deliver the video to global viewers using the AWS Global Edge Network. For live events, customers can deliver live streaming video using a live video encoder, like AWS Elemental MediaLive, to transcode the video into live streaming formats, a scalable origin to serve the video, like AWS Elemental MediaStore, and CloudFront to deliver the live video to a global audience.

Continue learning about CloudFront for Media & Entertainment use cases by browsing the CloudFront for Media and Entertainment web page at aws.amazon.com/cloudfront/media/.

Describe DNS

Resources on a network are assigned IP addresses used to locate and communicate with each other. IP addresses can be difficult to remember and don't provide meaning to a user when the user needs to remember how to access a resource. Domain Name System (DNS) is a service that uses name servers to translate a user-friendly domain name to the IP address assigned to a resource. DNS services can be experienced in action by visiting a website, such as aws.amazon.com. When aws.amazon.com is entered into the address bar, the web browser communicates with the DNS name servers that store the domain name aws.amazon.com. Then, the name servers provide the IP address associated with aws.amazon.com to the web browser, and the browser uses the IP address to find the web server that hosts the AWS website. Finally, the browser loads the AWS website from the web server and the site can be browsed freely.

Continue learning about DNS by browsing the What is DNS? web page web page at aws.amazon.com/route53/what-is-dns/.

Describe Amazon Route 53

Amazon Route 53 is a cloud DNS web service enabling users to visit websites and Internet applications using a user-friendly name. Route 53 performs three primary functions: registering domain names, routing Internet traffic to resources in a domain, and checking the health of resources. To improve user experience and ensure websites and web applications are easily accessible on the Internet, a domain name, such as amazon.com, can be registered for the site or app with a domain registrar. To register a domain name with Route 53, customers first choose a name and verify it is available. Then, they register the domain name providing the name and contact information of the domain owner. Route 53 then sends the information to the domain registrar on behalf of the customer. If a customer has already registered the domain name with a registrar, they can transfer the domain to Route 53 or simply add the domain to begin routing traffic to resources in the domain. To begin routing traffic to resources, customers create a record for each resource in the domain with a user-friendly name, such as aws.amazon.com. When a customer enters the name in a web browser, Route 53 will route the traffic to the resource enabling the browser to display the content provided by the resource. With Route 53, customers can create health checks to continuously check the health status of resources in the domain. Customers can view the health status of resources in the Route 53 console, or they can configure notifications to set a CloudWatch alarm to automatically notify them when an unhealthy resource is detected. Route 53 health checks together with the DNS failover feature can be configured to automatically failover an unhealthy resource to a healthy resource that performs the same function.

Continue learning about Amazon Route 53 by browsing the Amazon Route 53 web page at aws.amazon.com/route53/.

Describe AWS VPN

A virtual private network (VPN) is a security mechanism that creates a secure network connection between devices through the Internet. A VPN encrypts data and hides the IP address of devices to safely and anonymously transfer data between devices. AWS VPN is a remote access solution enabling customers to connect their on-premises networks, remote offices, and client devices with their AWS environments. AWS VPN offers two types of virtual private network services: Client VPN and Site-to-Site VPN. Client VPN is a fully managed remote access service enabling remote client devices to connect to AWS and on-premises corporate networks. Customers commonly use Client VPN to allow remote users to access resources, applications, and data hosted in their AWS and on-premises environments. Customers also use Client VPN to enable user access to applications after migrating to the Cloud and to securely connect IoT devices to AWS and on-premises environments. Site-to-Site VPN is a fully managed remote access service enabling customers to connect their on-premises data centers to their AWS environments. Customers commonly use Site-to-Site VPN to seamlessly migrate applications and IT resources to the AWS Cloud. After migration, Site-to-Site VPN enables on-premises applications and resources to continue using the apps and resources in the Cloud just as they did when they were on site.

Continue learning about AWS VPN by browsing the AWS VPN web page at aws.amazon.com/vpn/.

Identify resources for technology support

List the four types of AWS technical support plans

AWS offers five different technical support plans: Basic, Developer, Business, Enterprise On-Ramp, and Enterprise. Each support plan offers access to different tools and technical expertise and are billed at different price levels. The primary differences between the support plans include when and how customers can contact support, the level of AWS personnel providing support, available Trusted Advisor best practice checks, response time for impaired systems, depth of architectural guidance provided, third-party software support, access to architectural, scaling, and operational support for planned events, access to a TAM and the Concierge Support Team, and price per month.

Continue learning about the AWS Support Plans by browsing the Compare AWS Support Plans web page at aws.amazon.com/premiumsupport/plans/.

Describe the AWS Basic Support plan

The Basic Support plan is included with all AWS accounts free of charge. The plan provides customers access to customer service for account and billing questions but provides no access to technical or architectural support. The plan includes access to public self-help documentation, such as AWS whitepapers, support forums, user guides, and developer guides. All service limits Trusted Advisor checks and six core security checks are included in the plan to provide guidance on improving security of the AWS environment: Amazon S3 Bucket Permissions, Security Groups - Specific Ports Unrestricted, AWS IAM Use, MFA on root account, Amazon EBS Public Snapshots, Amazon RDS Public Snapshots. The plan provides customers with access to the AWS Health Dashboard with a personalized view of the health of their AWS resources. AWS only recommends Basic Support for customers that are becoming familiar with AWS services and have no resources in testing or production environments.

Continue learning about the AWS Basic Support plan by browsing the Compare AWS Support Plans web page at aws.amazon.com/premiumsupport/plans/.

Describe the AWS Developer Support plan

The AWS Developer Support plan is ideal for customers who are experimenting, developing, or testing AWS resources or applications in the AWS Cloud. AWS does not recommend Developer Support for customers who have resources in a production environment. The plan allows one contact in the AWS account to open an unlimited number of technical support cases with AWS Support via email and receive support during normal business hours, 8:00 AM to 6:00 PM in the customer's country. Developer Support is the minimum plan customers need to receive general guidance support within 24 hours and receive technical support for impaired systems within 12 hours from a Cloud Support Associate. It is also the minimum plan customers need to gain access to self-service resource management automations created by the AWS Support team. With Developer Support, customers have access to building-block architecture support to provide general guidance on how AWS services, resources, and features can work together. Developer Support includes the same service limits and six core security Trusted Advisor checks included with Basic Support and access to the AWS Health Dashboard. Billing for the Developer Support plan is the greater of $29 per month or 3% of the monthly AWS usage for the account.

Continue learning about the AWS Developer Support plan by browsing the AWS Developer Support web page at aws.amazon.com/premiumsupport/plans/developers/.

Describe the AWS Business Support plan

The AWS Business Support plan is the minimum recommended support plan for customers who are running production workloads in the AWS Cloud. Business Support is the minimum recommended plan required for customers to receive the following support features, access to all Trusted Advisor best practice checks, an unlimited number of contacts can open support cases with AWS Support, cases can be opened via phone, email, and chat, support is received 24 hours a day, 7 days a week, support provided by a Cloud Support Engineer, Identity and Access Management support, technical support within 4 hours for production systems that are impaired and within 1 hour for production systems that are down, architectural guidance based on the customer's use case, the ability to manage support cases programmatically with the AWS Support API, interoperability and configuration support for third-party software, and architecture and scaling guidance and operational support during the preparation and execution of planned events for an additional fee. Business Support also includes the same general guidance support within 24 hours and technical support for impaired non-production systems within 12 hours as the Developer Support plan. Billing for the Business Support plan is the greater of $100 per month or the sum of 10% of monthly AWS usage for the first $10K, 7% of usage from $10K-$80K, 5% of usage from $80K-$250K, and 3% of usage over $250K.

Continue learning about the AWS Business Support plan by browsing the AWS Business Support web page at aws.amazon.com/premiumsupport/plans/business/.

Describe the AWS Enterprise On-Ramp Support plan

The AWS Enterprise On-Ramp Support plan is the minimum recommended support plan for customers who are running production and business critical workloads in the AWS Cloud. Enterprise On-Ramp Support is the minimum recommended plan required for customers to receive the following support features, technical support from AWS Support within 30 minutes for business-critical systems that are down, application architecture guidance for their specific use case, workload, or application, architecture and scaling guidance and operational support during the preparation and execution of one planned event per year included in the monthly price of the plan, access to a pool of Technical Account Managers (TAMs) to provide proactive guidance, and access to the Concierge Support Team for billing and account support. Enterprise On-Ramp Support includes the same general guidance support within 24 hours, technical support for impaired non-production systems within 12 hours, support for impaired productions systems within 4 hours, and support for productions systems that are down within 1 hour as the Business Support plan. Billing for the Enterprise On-Ramp Support plan is the greater of $5,500 per month or 10% of the monthly AWS usage for the account.

Continue learning about the AWS Enterprise On-Ramp Support plan by browsing the AWS Enterprise On-Ramp web page at aws.amazon.com/premiumsupport/plans/enterprise-onramp/.

Describe the AWS Enterprise Support plan

The AWS Enterprise Support plan is ideal for customers who are running business and mission critical workloads in the AWS Cloud. Enterprise Support is the minimum recommended plan required for customers to receive the following support features, technical support from AWS Support within 15 minutes for business-critical and mission-critical systems that are down, architecture and scaling guidance and operational support during the preparation and execution of unlimited planned events included in the monthly price of the plan, access to proactive reviews, workshops, and deep dives, access to a designated Technical Account Manager (TAM) to proactively monitor the AWS environment, and access to online self-paced training labs. Enterprise Support includes the same general guidance support within 24 hours, technical support for impaired non-production systems within 12 hours, support for impaired productions systems within 4 hours, and support for production systems that are down within 1 hour as the Business and Enterprise On-Ramp Support plans. Billing for the Enterprise Support plan is the greater of $15,000 per month or the sum of 10% of monthly AWS usage for the first $150K, 7% of usage from $150K-$500K, 5% of usage from $500K-$1M, and 3% of usage over $1M.

Continue learning about the AWS Enterprise Support plan by browsing the AWS Enterprise Support web page at aws.amazon.com/premiumsupport/plans/enterprise/.

Create an AWS Support case

Customers can create a support case using the AWS Support Center in the AWS Management Console. After logging in to the Console, a customer selects Support in the upper right corner, selects Support Center, and selects Create case. Next, the customer must select the type of case to create: Account and billing support, Service limit increase, or Technical support. Then, the customer selects or enters the information needed to create the case, such as the service that is impacted, the severity level of the issue, and a description of the issue. After the case is created, an AWS Support representative will contact the customer within the time frame designated for the severity of the case and the support plan the customer has purchased. For the case type, customers with a Basic Support plan cannot select Technical support. For the case severity, customers with a Developer Support plan can select General guidance (1-day response time) or System impaired (12-hour response time. Customers with a Business Support plan can choose the same severity as a Developer Support plan as well as Production system impaired (4-hour response) or Production system down (1-hour response). Customers with an Enterprise On-Ramp or an Enterprise Support plan can choose the same severity as a Business Support plan as well as Business-critical system down (30-minute response) for Enterprise On-Ramp and Business-critical system down (15-minute response) for Enterprise Support.

Continue learning about creating an AWS Support case by reading the Getting started with AWS Support, Creating support cases and case management section of the AWS Support User Guide.

Describe AWS Trusted Advisor

AWS Trusted Advisor is a support tool and console providing customers with best practice checks and guidance to optimize their AWS environment by improving security, fault tolerance, and performance, reducing overall costs, and monitoring service usage and limits. Trusted Advisor analyzes a customer's AWS environment and compares it to AWS performance, fault tolerance, security, and cost optimization, best practices and compares a customer's service usage with service limits. Based on the comparisons, Trusted Advisor makes recommendations to increase availability and redundancy, improve performance and security, and optimize cost of resources deployed in the AWS Cloud. With an AWS Basic Support or Developer Support plan, a customer does not have access to any performance, fault tolerance, or cost optimization checks. They do have access to six core security checks and all 51 service limits checks. Customers with a Business Support, Enterprise On-Ramp Support, or Enterprise Support plan have access to all 20 cost optimization, 11 performance, 23 fault tolerance, 20 security, and 51 service limits checks.

Continue learning about AWS Trusted Advisor by browsing the AWS Trusted Advisor web page at aws.amazon.com/premiumsupport/technology/trusted-advisor/.

Describe the AWS Health Dashboard

The AWS Health Dashboard provides customers with a personalized view into events that may impact the performance and availability of AWS services and the underlying infrastructure that hosts their AWS resources. Customers can configure alerts to be sent to an email address or mobile phone in the event maintenance is planned for AWS infrastructure hosting the AWS Cloud. Alerts include details on how to remediate issues, restore service, and decrease the impact AWS maintenance has on customers' AWS environments. The AWS Health Dashboard is available to all AWS accounts regardless of the support plan purchased.

Continue learning about the AWS Health Dashboard by browsing the AWS Health Dashboard web page at aws.amazon.com/premiumsupport/technology/aws-health-dashboard/.

Describe the AWS Trust & Safety team

The AWS Trust & Safety team is dedicated to investigating and attempting to resolve incidents in which AWS resources are being used for abusive behavior. AWS considers any of the following types of behavior to be abusive, spam, port scanning, denial-of-service (DoS) attacks, intrusion attempts, hosting prohibited content, and distributing malware. Any AWS resources that are suspected of abusive behaviors are considered to be in violation of the AWS Terms of Service and should be reported to the Trust & Safety team. Abusive behavior should not be reported by opening a support case. Instead, anybody that suspects AWS resources are being used to engage in abusive behavior should contact the Trust & Safety team using the Report Amazon AWS abuse form or by emailing abuse@amazonaws.com.

Continue learning about the AWS Trust & Safety team and reporting abusive behavior by browsing the Report abuse of AWS resources web page at aws.amazon.com/premiumsupport/knowledge-center/report-aws-abuse/.

Describe the AWS Partner Network

The AWS Partner Network (APN) is a global community of trusted organizations and individuals that build, market, and sell AWS offerings enabling customers to accelerate their AWS Cloud journey. The APN community includes over 100,000 partners from more than 150 countries. When a partner joins the APN, they choose from the following partner paths that align with their customer offerings, software, hardware, services, training, and distribution. Then, the partner uses APN training and resources to gain expertise, earn partner badges, and validate their offerings to begin marketing and selling them with the AWS Marketplace. APN partners are measured against a high technical bar assuring the offerings from partners are trusted, provide value, and will help AWS customers move their business forward.

Continue learning about the AWS Partner Network by browsing the Work with an AWS Partner web page at aws.amazon.com/partners/work-with-partners/.

Describe AWS Marketplace

AWS Marketplace is an online catalog of software products and services sold by individuals, independent software vendors, managed services providers, and qualified APN partners. Customers can purchase software solutions from Marketplace to simplify procurement, provisioning, and governance of third-party software for their AWS environment. Customers can also purchase partner services to assist with configuring, deploying, and managing their third-party software. Marketplace includes over 12,000 products across 65 popular software categories, such as Operating Systems, Security, and Networking. The following product types can be sold and purchased on AWS Marketplace, AMI-based products, container-based products,

AWS Marketplace for Desktop Applications (AMDA), machine learning products, professional services, SaaS products, and data products. Some products on Marketplace are offered for free or as a free trial. Others are billed by AWS to the customer's account based on an hourly, monthly, annual, multi-year, or bring your own license pricing model. AWS handles paying the seller for any products customers buy on Marketplace.

Continue learning about AWS Marketplace by browsing the AWS Marketplace | Overview web page at aws.amazon.com/mp/marketplace-service/overview/.

Describe AWS Managed Services

AWS Managed Services (AMS) is a customer enablement service in which AWS operates and manages customers' infrastructure in their AWS environment. AMS enables customers to focus less on operating infrastructure and more on building their business and developing applications. AMS offers two operations plans: Accelerate and Advanced. With the AMS Accelerate operations plan, customers can engage AWS to perform day-to-day infrastructure operations tasks, such as monitoring and alerting, incident management, security management, and backup management. AMS Accelerate does not include operations services for provisioning AWS resources. With the AMS Advanced operations plan, customers can engage AWS for full-lifecycle services to provision, run, and support their AWS infrastructure. Full-life cycle services AMS Advanced provides include infrastructure changes and provisioning, access management, endpoint security, landing zone management, and all of the day-to-day operations services included with AMS Accelerate. AMS operations plans include operations services for infrastructure only and do not include services for application development, deployment, testing, or management. AMS is commonly used by customers to accelerate migrating their on-premises infrastructure to the AWS Cloud, to leverage a standard turnkey AWS cloud operating model, and to augment their staff when they don't have in-house cloud operations expertise.

Continue learning about AWS Managed Services by browsing the AWS Managed Services web page at aws.amazon.com/managed-services/.

Describe AWS Professional Services

AWS Professional Services is a customer enablement service in which AWS works alongside the customer and their chosen AWS partner to help the customer adopt the AWS Cloud. The AWS Professional Services global team provides a collection of offerings to deliver a set of activities, best practices, and documentation to help the customer achieve specific outcomes related to enterprise cloud adoption. AWS Professional Services also offers specialty services to assist customers in specific areas of enterprise cloud computing, such as analytics, application migration, application modernization, and blockchain. Customers commonly engage AWS Professional Services to accelerate digital transformation, help with large scale migrations for data center closures, and assist with innovative application development.

Continue learning about AWS Professional Services by browsing the AWS Professional Services web page at aws.amazon.com/professional-services/.

Describe AWS Training and Certification

AWS Training and Certification is a customer enablement service in which customers can purchase training to build cloud skills across their organization, and individuals can attain certifications to validate their expertise in various roles and specialties while working in the AWS Cloud. AWS Training and Certification offers customers many ways to learn about the Cloud, including digital courses, classroom training, partner provided training, and online or in-person events. AWS Training and Certification also offers customers a free Learning Needs Analysis to identify cloud skills gaps, and create a customized training and certification plan for the organization. Customers commonly use AWS Training and Certification to build cloud fluency throughout the organization, attract, develop, and retain top talent, and create a culture of innovation.

Continue learning about AWS Training and Certification by browsing the Team Training | Training and Certification web page at aws.amazon.com/training/enterprise/.

Locate AWS user guides, developer guides, and API references

AWS provides well organized public documentation on their website, including user guides, developer guides, API references, and tutorials. Using the documentation, anybody can learn how to do anything they want by simply looking through the documentation related to the AWS service they are working with and researching. To find the user guides and other documentation, visit the AWS website at aws.amazon.com, hover over Documentation, and select View all Documentation. On the AWS Documentation web page, links to the documentation for each AWS service are organized into service categories, such as Compute, Storage, and Database. Simply select the service you are working with or want to learn about, and you will find links to the documentation for the service.

Continue learning about the available AWS documentation by visiting the AWS Documentation web page at docs.aws.amazon.com/. Then, select a service you are interested in, and select the document and format that best suits your needs.

Locate AWS whitepapers

AWS whitepapers are documents that contain technical content written by AWS and the AWS community meant to expand customers' knowledge of AWS and provide insights into successfully operating and developing in the AWS Cloud. To find AWS whitepapers, visit the AWS website at aws.amazon.com, hover over Explore More, and select AWS Whitepapers & Guides. Another way to find whitepapers is to visit the AWS website, hover over Documentation, select View all Documentation, scroll to the General Resources section at the bottom of the page, and select AWS Whitepapers. A third way to find whitepapers is to visit the AWS website, select the magnifying class icon in the navigation menu, search for AWS whitepapers, and select AWS Whitepapers & Guides.

Continue learning about the available AWS whitepapers by visiting the AWS Whitepapers & Guides web page at aws.amazon.com/whitepapers/. Then, use the search and filter functionality to quickly find whitepapers you are interested in.

Describe the Cloud Computing Concepts Hub

The Cloud Computing Concepts Hub is a web page on the AWS website in which anybody can browse or search for articles that define and describe common concepts in cloud computing. The Concepts Hub includes articles for the most basic cloud computing concepts, like what is computer networking and what is an instance, to advanced concepts, like what is RESTful API and what is blockchain technology. The Concepts Hub is a great resource to refer to when learning about any new concepts in cloud computing.

Access the Cloud Computing Concepts Hub at aws.amazon.com/what-is/ and refer back to it anytime you come across a concept in cloud computing you are not familiar with.

Security and Compliance
Exam Domain

Define the AWS shared responsibility model

Describe what AWS means by shared responsibility

Shared responsibility refers to AWS and the customer both being responsible for the security and compliance of different aspects of the AWS Cloud resources. There is a clear divide between what AWS is responsible for securing and what the customer is responsible for securing.

Continue learning about the AWS shared responsibility model by reading the Security Foundations, Shared Responsibility section of the Security Pillar - AWS Well-Architected Framework whitepaper.

Identify which resources AWS is responsible for securing

AWS is responsible for security 'of' the cloud. AWS operates the infrastructure hosting the AWS Cloud services. Therefore, AWS is responsible for securing the global infrastructure in the Regions, Availability Zones, and Edge Locations, including compute, storage, database, and networking components. AWS is also responsible for securing the facilities the components reside in and any software that runs on the infrastructure, such as operating systems and virtualization software.

Continue learning about the resources AWS is responsible for securing by reading the Security of the AWS Infrastructure section of the Introduction to AWS Security whitepaper.

Identify which resources the AWS customer is responsible for securing

The customer is responsible for security 'in' the cloud. The customer operates the resources they provision with AWS Cloud services. Any data the customer creates or migrates to the cloud should be protected by the customer by implementing networking traffic protection, client-side and server-side encryption, data integrity checks, authentication and authorization measures, and managing encryption keys and SSL/TLS certificates. The customer is responsible for configuring firewalls and patching operating systems installed on any EC2 instances they launch in the AWS Cloud. The customer is also responsible for configuring Identity and Access Management to enforce who and what can access their AWS cloud resources and what permissions they have while accessing them.

Continue learning about the resources the AWS customer is responsible for securing by browsing the Shared Responsibility Model web page at aws.amazon.com/compliance/shared-responsibility-model/.

Define encryption

Encryption is a process used to keep data secure by encrypting, or scrambling, data rendering it impossible to read by any entity except for authorized users or resources. Decryption is the reverse process of encryption in which encrypted data is decrypted, or unscrambled, rendering the data readable. When data is encrypted, the encryption process uses an algorithm, such as AES-256, in combination with an encryption key to encrypt the data. The decryption process uses the same algorithm and either the same encryption key or a related key in a key pair to decrypt the data. Only the users and resources that are authorized to access the encryption key, or key pair, can decrypt and read the encrypted data. Great care must be taken to ensure encryption keys are only accessible by the entities that require access to the data protected by the keys. Most often encryption keys are managed and stored securely in a centralized system called a key management server, or KMS. AWS offers a service named AWS Key Management Service (KMS) which enables customers to securely manage and store encryption keys in the AWS Cloud.

Continue learning about encryption by reading The Importance of encryption and how AWS can help blog at aws.amazon.com/blogs/security/importance-of-encryption-and-how-aws-can-help/.

Identify who is responsible for encrypting data in transit

Data in transit, often called data in motion, refers to data as it moves from one component on a network to another. Because AWS owns and operates the physical hardware the data travels through, AWS is responsible for encrypting data in transit between resources within the AWS Cloud. However, it is the responsibility of the customer to encrypt any data in transit between AWS resources and resources outside of the AWS Cloud, such as data stored in an S3 bucket that is accessed by web clients and on-premises servers. For many AWS storage services, customers can enable features to ensure data is encrypted while in transit between the external client and the AWS Cloud. For example, AWS customers can enable the feature of an S3 bucket called client-side encryption to ensure data is encrypted while in transit between the client and the bucket. For customers with many AWS resources that are accessed by on-premises clients, AWS VPN is a great option to ensure data in transit is encrypted between environments. AWS VPN is a service dedicated to ensuring connections are secure and data is encrypted as it travels between a customer's AWS environment and their on-premises environment. AWS customers can create a Site-to-Site VPN to connect their on-premises networks to their AWS virtual private clouds ensuring data in transit is encrypted between both networks. Alternately, customers can create a Client VPN to grant their users access to AWS resources and encrypt data traveling between the AWS Cloud and the user's device.

Continue learning about the responsibility of encrypting data in transit by reading the Protecting your Data on AWS, Encrypt Data in Transit section of the of the Navigating GDPR Compliance on AWS whitepaper.

Identify who is responsible for encrypting data at rest

Data at rest refers to data as it is stored on a non-volatile storage device, such as a hard disk drive or solid-state drive. Customers are responsible for encrypting data at rest as it is stored with any AWS storage services, such as Amazon S3 and Amazon EBS. Customers are also responsible for encrypting data at rest with any AWS database services, such as Amazon RDS and Amazon Aurora. Although encrypting data at rest is the responsibility of the customer, some AWS services encrypt data at rest by default, such as DynamoDB. For other services, like Amazon S3, customers must enable encryption features, like server-side encryption, to encrypt data at rest as it is stored with the AWS service.

Continue learning about the responsibility of encrypting data at rest by reading the Protecting your Data on AWS, Encrypt Data at Rest section of the Navigating GDPR Compliance on AWS whitepaper.

Identify who is responsible for securing operating systems

The responsibility of securing operating systems in the AWS Cloud depends on which service the customer is using. For instances launched with Amazon EC2, the customer is responsible for securing the guest operating system running on the instance. This includes configuring who can access the operating system, securing traffic with firewalls, installing and operating antimalware solutions, and applying regular security patch updates. For AWS fully managed services, AWS is responsible for securing the operating system the provisioned resources run on, including these security tasks and all other management activities. Some common fully managed services in which AWS is responsible for securing the underlying operating systems includes Amazon RDS and Amazon Aurora for launching databases and Amazon ECS for running containers.

Continue learning about the responsibility of securing operating systems by reading the Security, Change management section of the Amazon Elastic Compute Cloud User Guide for Windows Instances.

Identify who is responsible for managing permissions

Permissions control who can access what and what they can do when they gain access. Customers are fully responsible for managing permissions to their AWS account and any resources they launch in the AWS Cloud. AWS Identify and Assessment Management (IAM) is a service that enables customers to control access and manage permissions to AWS accounts and resources by creating policies and attaching them to entities. With IAM, customers can configure identify based policies and attach them to users, groups, and roles to control which resources a user can access and what they can do when they access it. Customers can also configure resource-based policies and attach them to resources to control which users can access the resource and what they can do with it.

Continue learning about the responsibility of managing permissions by reading the Identity and access management, Permissions management section of the Security Pillar - AWS Well-Architected Framework whitepaper.

Identify who is responsible for complying with security related standards, laws, and regulations

The security related standards, laws, and regulations an organization must remain in compliance with depend on many factors, including which industry and sector the organization is in and where the organization does business. For example, public sector organizations commonly have to comply with the standards outlined in the NIST Cyber Security Framework, and healthcare organizations always have to remain in compliance with HIPAA regulations. It is the responsibility of AWS to ensure the global infrastructure the AWS Cloud runs on, the data center the infrastructure resides in, the people who deploy and operate the infrastructure, and the underlying infrastructure of fully managed services comply with security related standards, laws, and regulations required within the Region where the infrastructure resides as well as those outlined in the AWS Compliance Programs. It is the responsibility of the customer to ensure all operating systems, applications, services, and data installed on, created by, or stored in their AWS resources comply with security related standards, laws, and regulations. It is also the responsibility of the customer to train their staff and ensure they understand their compliance obligations.

Continue learning about the responsibility of complying with security related standards, laws, and regulations by reading the Compliance section of the Introduction to AWS Security whitepaper.

Define AWS Cloud security and compliance concepts

Describe the capabilities AWS offers for network and application protection

Network and application protection is the security concept of implementing security controls throughout a network ensuring workloads are protected against unauthorized access and potential vulnerabilities. AWS provides customers with many services and features to protect the infrastructure resources in their virtual private clouds (VPCs). Firewalls are security devices commonly used to protect infrastructure by monitoring traffic coming in and out of a network and allowing or blocking the traffic based on rules or patterns of activity recognized as potentially malicious. AWS Network Firewall is a network security service that enables customers to deploy firewalls to secure traffic coming in and out of their VPCs to ensure the infrastructure resources in their VPCs are protected. AWS Web Application Firewall (WAF) is an application security service that enables customers to secure their web applications by deploying firewalls on the networking and content delivery resources that enable communication with their applications, including Amazon CloudFront distributions, Application Load Balancers, Amazon API Gateway APIs, and AWS AppSync APIs. A DDoS attack is a distributed denial-of-service attack in which multiple devices or attackers launch a denial-of-service attack against a host, service, or application rendering the resource unusable by intended users. DDoS attacks can be devastating to an organization potentially causing huge losses in productivity and revenue. DDoS attacks cannot be prevented by most firewalls, so it is recommended to use security mechanisms that are purpose built to protect against DDoS attacks. AWS Shield is a security service dedicated to preventing DDoS attacks launched against customers' websites or applications.

Continue learning about the capabilities AWS offers for network and application protection by browsing the web page of each AWS service outlined in the Network and application section on the Cloud Security, Identity, and Compliance Products web page at aws.amazon.com/products/security/.

Describe a security group

A security group is similar to a host-based firewall for EC2 instances that is configured to allow traffic to and from instances based on traffic type, protocol, port range, and source or destination IP address. A security group is created in a VPC and can be associated with the network interface of any EC2 instance in the VPC. Each network interface can have up to five security groups associated with it. However, each security group can only be attached to one VPC and can only be associated with resources in the VPC it is attached to. When a VPC is created, a default security group is automatically created which allows all inbound and outbound traffic. Security groups are stateful, which means if traffic is allowed in the same traffic is allowed out of the VPC. If an AWS customer does not associate a security group with an EC2 instance, the default security group is automatically associated. The two primary differences between network ACLs and security groups are ACLs operate at the subnet level whereas security groups operate at the instance level, and ACLs support allow and deny rules whereas security groups support allow rules only.

Continue learning about security groups by reading the intro and Security groups basics in the Security, Security groups section of the Amazon Virtual Private Cloud User Guide.

Describe a network ACL

A network access control list (ACL) is similar to a network firewall and can be associated with subnets in a VPC to allow or deny EC2 instance traffic in to and out of the subnet. Each ACL can have multiple subnets associated with it, but each subnet can only be associated with one ACL. If a subnet is already associated with an ACL, and an AWS customer associates the subnet with a different ACL, the subnet is automatically disassociated from the original ACL. If customers don't associate an ACL with a subnet when it is created, a default ACL is created and associated. The default ACL allows all inbound and outbound traffic by default, but it can be modified by customers. Network ACL's can be modified by adding inbound rules for traffic coming in to instances in the VPC and outbound rules for traffic going out of the VPC. The rules are configured to either allow or deny traffic based on the type of traffic, protocol and port used, and the source IP address for inbound rules or the destination IP address for outbound rules. The two primary differences between network ACLs and security groups are ACLs operate at the subnet level whereas security groups operate at the instance level, and ACLs support allow and deny rules whereas security groups support allow rules only.

Continue learning about network ACLs by reading the intro and Network ACL basics in the Subnets, Network ACLs section of the Amazon Virtual Private Cloud User Guide.

Describe AWS WAF

A firewall is a filter that enables security and network administrators to control which traffic is blocked and which traffic is allowed into and out of a network based on conditions the administrator defines. Firewalls are used for security purposes to ensure resources in a network are protected against potential threats. AWS WAF is a web application firewall service enabling customers to protect their web applications from potential threats that could compromise the availability or security of the applications and data. Common web exploits WAF can help customers protect their web applications from include SQL injection and cross-site scripting (XSS) attacks. WAF lets customers control access to their web applications by monitoring requests forwarded to the following networking and content delivery resources, Amazon CloudFront distributions, Amazon API Gateway APIs, Application Load Balancers, and AWS AppSync APIs. With WAF, customers create rules to determine what WAF should do with the requests forwarded to the connectivity resources. In each rule, the customer configures the rule action, such as block or allow, and the rule statement with conditions like the IP address of the client that forwarded the request. Then, WAF compares each request to the rule statement, and if the request matches the conditions in the statement, WAF takes the configured rule action and blocks or allows the request to the web application.

Continue learning about AWS WAF by browsing the AWS WAF - Web Application Firewall web page at aws.amazon.com/waf/.

Describe AWS Shield

A denial-of-service attack is an attack which overloads a resource and prevents it from processing and responding to legitimate requests from users and clients. A distributed denial-of-service (DDoS) attack is a denial-of-service attack that is launched from multiple systems working together to send an influx of requests to a resource overloading it and preventing it from performing its intended purpose. AWS Shield is a security service dedicated to protecting a customer's applications running in the AWS Cloud from DDoS attacks. AWS offers two version of AWS Shield, Shield Standard and Shield Advanced. Shield Standard is automatically included for AWS customers at no additional charge and protects customer's applications from most common network and transport layer DDoS attacks. Shield Advanced is a paid for service that adds additional security and protects customer's applications from more sophisticated DDoS attacks. AWS recommends Shield Advanced for any applications that are access by users and clients across the Internet.

Continue learning about AWS Shield by browsing the AWS Shield web page at aws.amazon.com/shield/.

Describe AWS PrivateLink

AWS PrivateLink is a technology that enables customers to privately and securely connect their virtual private cloud (VPC) to AWS services outside of their VPC, including services in other AWS accounts and supported AWS Marketplace partner services. With PrivateLink, customers use a VPC endpoint to connect their VPC to outside services and enable AWS resources within and outside of their VPC to communicate with each other. VPC endpoints allow resources with private IP addresses in different VPC's to communicate with each other over the AWS network without using the Internet. Therefore, when customers use PrivateLink, they do not need to use other connectivity technology that enables communication over the internet, such as an internet gateway, NAT device, VPN connection, or AWS Direct Connect connection.

Continue learning more about AWS PrivateLink by browsing the AWS PrivateLink web page at aws.amazon.com/privatelink/.

Describe how customers can audit compliance of their AWS environment

A compliance audit is a comprehensive review of an organization's assets, operations, and business integrity to verify adherence to regulatory requirements that are mandated by compliance standards, laws, and regulations. AWS Audit Manager enables customers to continually audit their AWS environments for compliance with regulatory requirements. With Audit Manager, customers create an assessment and select a standard framework for the standards or regulations, such as GDPR or HIPAA, and the related controls they want to use to evaluate the compliance of their AWS environment. Alternately, customers can select a custom framework for the assessment and add the controls for their required standards, laws, and regulations. When customers create an assessment, they also select the AWS accounts and services they want to include and evaluate for compliance. When the assessment is created, Audit Manager automatically collects evidence from the accounts and services included in the assessment and evaluates the evidence against the controls in the selected framework. When the assessment is complete, Audit Manager creates an assessment report enabling the customer to view whether their policies, procedures, and activities are in compliance with required standards, laws, and regulations.

Continue learning about how customers can audit compliance of their AWS environments by browsing the AWS Audit Manager web page at aws.amazon.com/audit-manager/.

Define AWS Compliance Programs

In relation to security, regulatory compliance refers to taking steps to ensure a customer's data and information is secure in accordance with standard, laws, and regulations, such as GDPR which protects data in accordance with European data protection laws, PCI DSS which regulates compliance with Payment Card Industry Data Security Standards, and HIPAA which regulates compliance with the Health Insurance Portability and Accountability Act. AWS Compliance Programs are the set of policies, standards, procedures, and guidelines AWS has implemented to ensure the AWS Global Infrastructure, the data centers it resides in, and the people that operate it are in compliance with several standards, laws, and regulations. AWS maintains a web page of AWS Compliance Programs showing which standards, laws, and regulations AWS complies with and information on the controls in place within AWS to remain in compliance. Maintaining compliance is a shared responsibility between AWS and the customer. Customers can use the AWS Compliance Programs to share with auditors and regulators the steps AWS has taken to assure compliance. However, it is the responsibility of the customer to assure the AWS environment they provision and the data they store in the AWS Cloud maintain compliance with the standards, laws, and regulations to which they are required to adhere.

Continue learning about AWS Compliance Programs by browsing the Compliance Programs web page at aws.amazon.com/compliance/programs/.

Describe AWS Artifact

In IT, organizations often have to submit security and compliance documents to compliance auditors and regulators as proof of the controls in place assuring the organization is in compliance with standards, laws, and regulations. AWS Artifact is a console that enables customers to download security and compliance documents showing the measures AWS takes to assure the infrastructure, data centers, and people who operate them remain in compliance with standards, laws, and regulations. For example, customers can use the Artifact console to download AWS ISO certifications, Payment Card Industry (PCI) reports, and Service Organization Controls (SOC) reports and submit them to auditors and regulators as proof of compliance. With AWS Artifact, customers can also review, accept, and track compliance agreements to remain in compliance with certain laws and regulations, like the Health Insurance Portability and Accountability Act (HIPAA). Downloading reports and managing agreements with AWS Artifact is free of charge to AWS customers.

Continue learning about AWS Artifact by browsing the AWS Artifact web page at aws.amazon.com/artifact/.

Describe AWS Config

AWS Config is a configuration auditing service enabling customers to assess, audit, and evaluate the configurations of their AWS resources. With AWS Config, customers add rules to their account which are conditions they would like their AWS resources to meet. AWS includes managed rules customers can add to their account which are predefined specifications that must be met. For example, a customer can add the iam-password-policy AWS managed rule to their account, and Config will check if the IAM users in the account have a password policy that meets the requirements of the rule. Alternately, customers can create custom rules and manually configure the specifications that must be met by their AWS resources. After rules are added to the account, Config begins evaluating resources in the account against the rules and displays the rules, resources, and compliance state in the AWS Config Dashboard. Customers can use the Dashboard to identify rules and resources that are not in compliance and manually or automatically remediate the noncompliant resources.

Continue learning about AWS Config by browsing the AWS Config web page at aws.amazon.com/config/.

Describe Amazon Macie

Amazon Macie is a security service that enables customers to discover, monitor, and protect sensitive data in their AWS environment. Macie helps customers protect the security and privacy of sensitive data by automatically identifying personally identifiable information (PII) and financial data stored in S3 buckets. Macie evaluates the permissions and encryption status of objects in the buckets and creates detailed findings regarding the security and access control of the buckets in the customers

AWS environment. Customers can easily review the findings and take action to secure their sensitive data.

Continue learning about Amazon Macie by browsing the Amazon Macie web page at aws.amazon.com/macie/.

Identify Amazon S3 encryption options

Amazon S3 offers customers two options for encrypting data stored in S3 buckets, server-side encryption and client-side encryption. Server-side encryption automatically provides data at rest encryption as data is always encrypted by S3 servers before it is written to disk in AWS data centers. The data remains encrypted as it is stored and is decrypted by S3 before it is sent to a client requesting the object. Client-side encryption provides encryption of both data at rest and data in transit as the Amazon S3 Encryption Client encrypts an object before uploading the object to an S3 bucket. The object remains encrypted as it is stored on disks in AWS data centers. When a client requests the object, the object remains encrypted as it is sent to the client. When the client receives the object, it decrypts the object in order to read the data. With client-side encryption, the customer is responsible for managing the encryption process, encryption keys, and any related tools.

Continue learning about Amazon S3 encryption options by reading the Security, Data encryption section of the Amazon Simple Storage Service User Guide.

Identify Amazon EBS encryption options

Amazon EBS allows customers to enable encryption for a single volume or enable encryption by default for their AWS account to ensure every volume created in the account is encrypted. Encryption is supported for the EBS boot volume and data volumes of an EC2 instance, all volume types, all current generation instance types, and some previous generation instance types. When encryption is enabled for a volume, every snapshot created of the volume is also encrypted. Encryption cannot be enabled or disabled for existing volumes. EBS encryption uses AWS KMS keys when creating encrypted volumes and snapshots. To encrypt an unencrypted volume, customers can create a volume from an unencrypted snapshot and enable encryption when creating the volume. To decrypt an encrypted volume, customers can create a volume from an encrypted snapshot and disable encryption when creating the volume.

Continue learning about Amazon EBS encryption options by reading the Storage, Amazon EBS, EBS data services, EBS encryption section of the Amazon Elastic Compute Cloud User Guide for Windows Instances.

Identify Amazon RDS encryption options

To encrypt data at rest, AWS customers can enable encryption for an Amazon RDS DB instance when they create it. When encryption is enabled for a DB instance, the underlying storage volume is encrypted as well as any automated backups, read replicas, and snapshots. Data in transit between a DB instance and client applications can be encrypted using SSL/TLS. SSL/TLS encryption for data in transit is supported for the following RDS DB engines, Microsoft SQL Server, MariaDB, MySQL, PostgreSQL, and Oracle.

Continue learning about Amazon RDS encryption options by reading the Security, Data protection, Data encryption, Encrypting Amazon RDS resources section of the Amazon Relational Database Service User Guide.

Describe the capabilities AWS offers for identity and access control

Identity and access control is the security practice of managing users and resources as entities, managing authentication of the entities to prove their identity, and controlling what those entities have access to and what they can do when they are granted access. AWS has several services that enable customers to manage the identities of users and resources and the access granted to them in their AWS environment. AWS Identity and Access Management (IAM) is the service most commonly used by customers to create and manage user and machine identities in their AWS account. With IAM, customers can configure permissions to control which services and resources the identities can access and the operations they are allowed to perform on the resource. IAM is offered to AWS customers free of charge. AWS Directory Service is a fully managed Microsoft Active Directory service enabling customers to manage AWS Cloud user and resource identities and permissions. AWS Directory Service can also be integrated with existing on-premises Microsoft Active Directory environments enabling single sign-on ensuring users only need to log in once to access both AWS and on-premises environments. AWS IAM Identity Center, previously SSO, is a service enabling customers to centrally manage identities and access management for multiple AWS accounts and cloud-based applications. With IAM Identity Center, customers can create identities or import existing identities from external identity providers and manage permissions for the identities granting them access to resources in other AWS accounts in the organization and commonly used cloud applications, such as Salesforce, Box, and Office 365.

Continue learning about the capabilities AWS offers for identity and access control by reading the Security Products and Features, Identity and Access Control section of the Introduction to AWS Security whitepaper.

Describe AWS Secrets Manager

A secret in IT security refers to the credentials used to authenticate an entity to prove their identity. Commonly used secrets include passwords, keys, and tokens. When applications need access to a database or other data store, they are required to use a secret to authenticate with the data store and access the data. Without a secrets management tool, the secret an application uses to access data is included in the applications source code. Including a secret in the code is a security risk because anybody who can view the code can also view the secret and use it to gain unauthorized access to confidential data. AWS Secrets Manager is a service that solves this issue. With Secrets Manager, customers can store credentials for multiple applications and data stores and use API calls to Secrets Manager in the source code of applications instead of hard coding the secrets. Secrets Manager also enables customers to automatically rotate secrets on a schedule reducing the risk of compromised credentials.

Continue learning about AWS Secrets Manager by browsing the AWS Secrets Manager web page at aws.amazon.com/secrets-manager/.

Describe AWS Certificate Manager

An SSL/TLS certificate is a file that contains authentication information about a user or device and encryption keys used for secure communication. A certificate is created by a certificate authority (CA) and digitally signed by the CA proving the identity of the user or device. When a certificate is created for a device, it must be installed in a certificate store on the device. After it is installed, the certificate is used to secure the communication between the device and other devices or users. The communication is secured by using the certificate to prove the identity of the device, sharing the encryption key with the destination device, and encrypting the data before sending it over the network. AWS Certificate Manager (ACM) is a service that simplifies the process of creating, managing, and deploying SSL/TLS certificates for AWS resources to secure communication across the Internet or with on-premises networks. ACM acts as the certificate authority and enables customers to easily request certificates for their AWS resources. ACM reduces manual efforts by automatically deploying certificates to resources and renewing certificates when they retire. AWS regularly adds support for more services to ACM. Currently, ACM certificates are supported by Elastic Load Balancing, Amazon CloudFront, Amazon Cognito, AWS Elastic Beanstalk, AWS App Runner, Amazon API Gateway, AWS Nitro Enclaves, AWS CloudFormation, AWS Amplify, and Amazon OpenSearch Service.

Continue learning about AWS Certificate Manager by browsing the AWS Certificate Manager web page at aws.amazon.com/certificate-manager/.

Describe the tools AWS offers for monitoring and logging

Monitoring and logging are the security practices of tracking activities that occur in an environment to detect and respond to security incidents and prevent them from occurring again in the future. AWS offers many tools for monitoring and logging security incidents in AWS environments enabling customers to identify issues before they disrupt service or compromise the confidentiality or integrity of their workloads and data. AWS CloudTrail is an activity logging service enabling customers to monitor their AWS environment and verify who or what is accessing their cloud resources. CloudTrail reports on what the potential attacker is doing, when they are doing it, and from where they are doing it. Amazon CloudWatch is an event logging service that gathers logs, metrics, and events from AWS resources and applications deployed customers' AWS and on-premises environments. CloudWatch provides customers with a comprehensive view into the status of their AWS and on-premises workloads allowing them to take manual or automated actions to remediate threats and potentially malicious activity. Amazon GuardDuty is a threat detection service that monitors activity in an AWS environment for signs of malicious activity and unauthorized access. GuardDuty continuously presents findings to customers enabling them to take immediate action and remediate a potential attack.

Continue learning about the tools AWS for monitoring and logging by reading the Security Products and Features, Monitoring and Logging section of the Introduction to AWS Security whitepaper.

Describe VPC Flow Logs

VPC Flow Logs is a feature of Amazon VPC which enables customers to log all network traffic in a virtual private cloud (VPC), including traffic between network interfaces in the VPC and external networks. AWS customers can create a flow log for a VPC, a subnet, or a network interface to capture and monitor IP traffic from a single interface or all network interfaces in a subnet or VPC. Flow logs can be configured to store or publish captured log data to an Amazon CloudWatch Logs log group or an Amazon S3 bucket. The captured log data includes multiple fields showing the AWS account ID of the owner of the network interface that initiated the traffic, the IP address of the interface that initiated the traffic, the IP address of the interface that received the traffic, the protocol and port used, the number of packets and bytes transferred, the time of the transmission, and much more.

Continue learning about VPC flow logs by reading the intro and Flow logs basics in the Monitoring, VPC Flow Logs section of the Amazon Virtual Private Cloud User Guide.

Describe AWS CloudTrail

AWS CloudTrail is a log monitoring and user tracking service enabling customers to monitor and audit the governance and compliance of their AWS account. CloudTrail automatically stores a history of user and resource activity by recording API calls made on an AWS account. The activity and event history can be used to identify compliance issues, investigate security incidents, fulfill compliance auditor requests, and track what users are doing with resources in an AWS environment. CloudTrail provides visibility into the activity of users and resources in an AWS environment by storing an audit trail of changes and other actions in the environment. The audit trail shows from which account and IP address the action occurred as well as the data and time it occurred. CloudTrail can be configured to automatically respond to an action when it occurs, or customers can respond manually after investigating the audit trail.

Continue learning about AWS CloudTrail by browsing the AWS CloudTrail web page at aws.amazon.com/cloudtrail/.

Describe Amazon CloudWatch

Amazon CloudWatch is a monitoring and observability service enabling customers to monitor, analyze, and troubleshoot their AWS resources and applications. CloudWatch gathers monitoring and operational data, such as logs, metrics, and events, from resources and applications in the AWS Cloud and on premises. CloudWatch presents monitoring and operational data to customers in dashboards enabling the visualization of applications and infrastructure, correlation of events, and analysis of metrics and logs. Customers use CloudWatch to gain insight into the health status of their environment and improve operational performance and resource optimization. CloudWatch alarms can be created to notify customers of potential issues or other information of interest or to automatically trigger actions with other AWS services based on metrics, such as triggering Auto Scaling to automatically remove or add EC2 instances when CPU utilization reaches a certain percentage.

Continue learning about Amazon CloudWatch by browsing the Amazon CloudWatch web page at aws.amazon.com/cloudwatch/.

Describe Amazon Inspector

Amazon Inspector is a vulnerability assessment service enabling customers to remediate threats and protect the reliability and security of their AWS workloads. Inspector automatically and continuously scans EC2 instances in the customer's AWS environment and any container images residing in Amazon Elastic Container Registry (ECR). When Inspector finds a vulnerability or potential security issue, it creates a finding with a description of the vulnerability, the affected resource, the severity of the vulnerability, and guidance on how to remediate the potential security issue. Customers can review the findings and take action to remediate the issue and prevent it from occurring again in the future.

Continue learning about Amazon Inspector by browsing the Amazon Inspector web page at aws.amazon.com/inspector/.

Describe Amazon GuardDuty

A threat in cybersecurity is any activity or condition that could negatively impact an organization and technologies through unauthorized access, destruction, disclosure of confidential information, modification of data, or denial of service. Amazon GuardDuty is a threat detection service that enables customers to mitigate the risk of threats impacting the confidentiality, integrity, and availability of workloads and data in the AWS Cloud. GuardDuty analyzes data from AWS CloudTrail management and event logs, VPC Flow Logs, CloudTrail S3 data event logs, and DNS logs to detect unauthorized and unexpected activity. GuardDuty uses threat intelligence feeds with known malicious IP addresses and domains and machine learning to identify potentially malicious activity. Customers can use the GuardDuty findings to investigate potential threats and take action to mitigate the risk of the threat impacting the confidentiality, integrity, and availability of their workloads and data in their AWS environment.

Continue learning about Amazon GuardDuty by browsing the AWS GuardDuty web page at aws.amazon.com/guardduty/.

Describe Amazon Detective

Amazon Detective is a security service that enables customers to analyze and visualize data to identify the root cause of potentially malicious activity and security issues. Detective automatically gathers login attempts, API calls, and network traffic from AWS CloudTrail and VPC flow logs and findings detected by GuardDuty. Detective stores and analyzes one year's worth of the gathered security data, analyzes changes in the type and volume of activity over time, and presents customers with visualizations of the findings and potential security issues. Customers use the visualizations to easily investigate security issues and find the root cause to mitigate risk and prevent the issue from occurring again in the future.

Continue learning about Amazon Detective by browsing the Amazon Detective web page at aws.amazon.com/detective/.

Identify AWS access management capabilities

Define access management

Access management in IT, also called access control, is a security methodology used to verify the identity of users and other entities, control which resources an entity can access, and restrict what they can do when accessing them. There are two primary practices included in access management, authentication and authorization.

Continue learning about what access management is by reading the What is the difference between identity management and access management? section on the What is Identity Management? web page at vmware.com/topics/glossary/content/identity-management.html/.

Define authentication

Authentication refers to a user or other entity providing credentials to prove their identity. Common credentials used to authenticate a user include passwords, PINs, and fingerprints. Multi-factor authentication is a practice that adds an additional layer of security by requiring a user to submit at least two different forms of authentication before they are granted access to a resource. In order to be considered multi-factor authentication, each form of authentication must meet a different factor, something you know, something you have, and something you are. Something you know refers to something that can be remembered, like a password or PIN. Something you have refers to something that can be possessed, like a smart card or authentication token. Something you are refers to biometrics, or parts of the body, like fingerprints or facial features.

Continue learning about what authentication is by browsing the Authentication Definition web page at techterms.com/definition/authentication.

Define authorization

Authorization refers to controlling what actions or level of access a user or other entity has when accessing a resource. An administrator configures permissions specifying which resources the entity can access and what they can do when accessing them. Common actions enforced by permissions include creating, deleting, and modifying objects.

Continue learning about what authorization is by browsing the What is Authorization and Access Control? web page at icann.org/en/blogs/details/what-is-authorization-and-access-control-2-12-2015-en/.

Describe AWS IAM

AWS IAM (Identity and Access Management) is an access control service that is free to use with every AWS account. The service enables an AWS customer to manage authentication and authorization for their AWS services and resources. With IAM, an AWS customer creates identities for users and AWS resources and assigns security credentials to authenticate the identity during log in or when it tries to access a resource. The customer also assigns permissions to the identity to authorize what AWS resources the identity can access and what actions it can perform when accessing them.

Continue learning about AWS IAM by browsing the AWS Identity & Access Management web page at aws.amazon.com/iam/.

Describe an IAM user

An IAM user is an entity customers create for authentication and authorization purposes in AWS IAM to represent a human, system, or application that interacts with the AWS Cloud. An IAM user consists of a name and credentials that can be used to sign in to the AWS Management Console or programmatically authenticate with AWS services. When customers create a user, three names are created to identify the user: a friendly name, an Amazon Resource Name (ARN), and a unique ID. A friendly name is the name customers specify when creating a user and is displayed in the Management Console. Each friendly name in an AWS account must be unique. An ARN is a name AWS assigns to each user that combines the AWS account ID and friendly name. The ARN is used to uniquely identify users across AWS for tasks like creating IAM policies. A unique ID is another name AWS assigns to uniquely identify each user. The ARN is more commonly used to uniquely identify a user, but the unique ID can be useful in specific cases, such as when a user is deleted from an account and the same friendly name is reused for a new user. Four types of credentials can be created for a user depending on how the user will interact with AWS services: a console password, an access key, an SSH key, and a server certificate. A console password is required for any user to sign in to the Management Console to interact with AWS services. An access key is a key pair that can be created for an IAM user representing an application, script, or developer enabling them to make programmatic requests to AWS resources. AWS recommends using an IAM role to assign temporary credentials and permissions to an application or script instead of assigning a long-term access key. An SSH key is a public-private key pair that can be used to authenticate users with CodeCommit repositories using the SSH protocol. Customers also use SSH keys to authenticate with Amazon EC2 instances when connecting via a command line interface. A server certificate is an SSL/TLS certificate that must be created for a user representing a web application to enable HTTPS connections with clients. When an IAM user is created using the Management Console, customers must create either a password or access key for the user. When a user is created using the CLI or API, no credentials are created by default. Customers must create credentials for the user before they can do anything with AWS services.

Continue learning about IAM users by reading the Identities, Users section of the AWS Identity and Access Management User Guide.

Describe an IAM policy

Permissions are the component of authorization that grant an identity the rights to perform actions when accessing a resource. With IAM, permissions can be assigned to users, groups, roles, or AWS resources by creating a policy and attaching it to the entity. Policies attached to an IAM user, group, or role are called identity-based policies, and they control which resources the users are authorized to access. Policies attached to an AWS resource are called resource-based policies, and they control which users or other resources are authorized to access the resource. An example of an IAM resource-based policy is a bucket policy created and attached to an S3 bucket to grant access permissions to the bucket and the objects created by the bucket owner. When attaching policies to an entity, customers can choose between AWS managed policies or customer managed policies. AWS managed policies are preconfigured with permissions that authorize users for many common use cases, such as granting full access to DynamoDB resources to a database administrator. AWS managed policies are often referred to simply as managed policies, and they cannot be changed by a customer. Customer managed policies, often referred to as custom policies, are policies customers can add permission to granting entities access to resources for their specific use case.

Continue learning about IAM policies by browsing the IAM Fine-Grained Access Control web page at aws.amazon.com/iam/features/manage-permissions/.

Describe an IAM user group

AWS customers can create IAM groups to manage the permissions for multiple users collectively instead of each user individually. By creating groups, customers can manage and control access for users that have a similar job role and responsibilities. When a new or existing user takes on the job role, they can be added to the group, and they will inherit the policies and permissions attached to the group. IAM groups are a great way of ensuring the principle of least privilege is applied to identity and access management practices.

Continue learning about IAM groups by reading the Identities, User groups section of the AWS Identity and Access Management User Guide.

Describe an IAM role

An IAM role is an identity designed to temporarily grant permissions to a user, resource, or application. IAM policies are configured and attached to an IAM role in the same way they are attached to users, user groups, and resources. When a role is created, the creator must grant entities permission to switch to the role in any policy attached to the entity before they can assume the role. Then when the entity needs additional permissions to perform certain actions with resources, the entity switches to the role, they inherit the policies attached to the role, and they can perform the necessary actions with the resources. After the entity logs out or disconnects from the resource, the role session is ended, and the entity will no longer have the permissions granted to the role.

Continue learning about IAM roles by reading the Identities, Roles section of the AWS Identity and Access Management User Guide.

Describe the concept of identity federation

Identity federation is the process of linking one identity management system, such as Microsoft Active Directory, in one environment with another identity management system in another environment. Identity federation ensures users stored in each identity management system can access resources in both environments. The user accounts in federated identity management systems are referred to as federated identities. AWS customers can implement identity federation to seamlessly authenticate and authorize accounts and applications across their AWS environment and other environments using two services, AWS SSO or AWS IAM.

Continue learning about identity federation by browsing the Identity federation in AWS web page at aws.amazon.com/identity/federation/.

Describe the principle of least privilege

The principle of least privilege states a user should only be given the permissions they need to do their job and no more. The principle ensures a user can't deliberately or accidentally perform an action that could cause damage to the confidentiality, integrity, or availability of resources and data. Applied to AWS, the principle of least privilege states a user should only be granted access to the cloud resources they need to do their job and should only be given permissions to perform the actions they need to be successful.

Continue learning about the principle of least privilege by reading Grant least privilege in the Security, Security best practices and use cases, Security best practices section of the AWS Identity and Access Management User Guide.

Describe multi-factor authentication

In the cybersecurity field, there are three different factors, or categories, of authentication: something you know, something you are, and something you have. Something you know refers to something that can be memorized, like a password or user created PIN. Something you are refers to a part of the body or behaviors, like fingerprints or typing patterns. Something you have refers to something that can be possessed, like a smart card or computer-generated token. Multi-factor authentication (MFA) is an authentication method in which an identity must be authenticated using at least two of the three factors of authentication. AWS recommends requiring MFA for all IAM users and the account root user to add an extra layer of security to the authentication process. In AWS, MFA can be enabled for each IAM user individually. Alternately, customers can enforce MFA requirements for IAM users and create a policy that allows the user to change their own credentials and manage their MFA devices. Before enabling MFA for an IAM user, the user must either purchase a supported hardware MFA device or install an MFA application on their smartphone. After a user has an MFA device, the device must be enabled for the IAM user. Once the MFA device is enabled, when the user logs in to their AWS account, their MFA device will receive a six-digit code. Then depending on the type of device, the user either enters the code or taps the device to complete the authentication process, the log in is successful, and access is granted to the authorized AWS services and resources.

Continue learning about multi-factor authentication by browsing the Multi-factor Authentication (MFA) for IAM web page at aws.amazon.com/iam/features/mfa/.

Describe the security best practice of password rotation

Password rotation, or rotating credentials, is a security best practice referring to changing a user's password on a regular basis. The goal of password rotation is to ensure credentials that are unknowingly compromised, or stolen, cannot be used by an attacker to continue accessing user's resources long term. AWS recommends configuring a password policy in the AWS account settings to enforce password rotation for all IAM users. To enforce a password rotation policy for all users, customers should configure two password policy options, enable password expiration and prevent password reuse. Enable password expiration should be set to the number of days before users are required to change their password. Prevent password reuse should be set to the number of passwords users must change before they can reuse an old password.

Continue learning about password rotation by reading Rotate credentials regularly in the Security, Security best practices and use cases, Security best practices section of the AWS Identity and Access Management User Guide.

Describe the AWS account root user

The AWS account root user is the AWS account owner and the first user automatically created when an AWS customer creates and activates a new AWS account. The root user has full access to all resources in the AWS account. However, AWS does not recommend using the root user for everyday tasks. Instead, AWS recommends creating an IAM user and granting them permissions to perform everyday tasks in the AWS Cloud. There are certain tasks that only the root user can perform. Those tasks are changing AWS account settings, restoring IAM user permissions, activating IAM access to the Billing and Cost Management console, viewing certain tax invoices, closing an AWS account, changing or cancelling an AWS support plan, registering as a seller in the Reserved Instance Marketplace, configuring an Amazon S3 bucket to enable MFA Delete, editing or deleting an S3 bucket policy that includes an invalid VPC ID or VPC endpoint ID, and signing up for GovCloud.

Continue learning about the AWS account root user by reading the AWS security credentials, AWS users section of the AWS General Reference Guide.

Describe how to protect the AWS account root user

The AWS account root user cannot be deleted or renamed. The best way to protect the account root user is to not use it for everyday tasks. If customers do use the root user, AWS recommends enabling multi-factor authentication (MFA) for the root user. Enabling MFA ensures anybody who logs in to the Management Console with the root user email address and password must also enter an authentication code generated with a virtual or hardware MFA device before access is granted. If a customer chooses to use the root user with the AWS CLI, SDK's, or API's, AWS recommends creating access keys for the root user to sign programmatic requests.

Continue learning about protecting the AWS account root user by reading Enable MFA on the AWS account root user and Creating access keys for the root user in the Identities, AWS account root user section of the AWS Identity and Access Management User Guide.

Describe S3 access points

An S3 access point is a feature of Amazon S3 that simplifies access management for S3 buckets. When developing in the AWS Cloud, it is common to use a single bucket to store data for multiple applications. The bucket policy attached to the bucket must be configured to grant the appropriate permissions to each app that accesses data in the bucket. As the bucket grows and more apps access the bucket, managing policies becomes increasingly complex. Instead of managing complex policies, customers can create an S3 access point for each app or group of apps that require the same permissions to the bucket. Then, customers can create access control policies for each access point granting the appropriate permissions to access the bucket and even grant access to specific objects within it. AWS customers can create and use S3 access points at no additional cost.

Continue learning about S3 access points by browsing the Amazon S3 Access Points web page at aws.amazon.com/s3/features/access-points/.

Describe S3 block public access

S3 block public access is a feature of Amazon S3 that enables customers to limit who can access their S3 buckets. When a bucket is created, only the bucket owner has access to the bucket by default. However, users can modify bucket policies, bucket ACLs, and object ACLs to grant public access to a bucket and the objects in it. Public access means anybody in the world can access the data stored in a bucket. Granting access to anybody in the world introduces potential threats and security risk to the AWS environment. The block public access feature can be enabled for a bucket, access point, or an entire AWS account to override any permissions that grant public access. The block public access feature allows account administrators and bucket owners to centrally manage authorization ensuring only known and intended users have access to the bucket.

Continue learning about S3 block public access by browsing the Amazon S3 Block Public Access web page at aws.amazon.com/s3/features/block-public-access/.

Describe Amazon Cognito

Amazon Cognito is a user management service enabling customers to provide authentication and authorization for their web and mobile applications. Cognito includes two components for authentication and authorization, user pools and identity pools. A user pool is a user directory enabling customers to use a built-in, customizable user interface for their users to sign up and sign in to their application. When a user signs up, a profile is created in the user pool enabling the user to sign in to the application going forward. User pools can also be configured to allow sign in with a social media account or an account hosted with a third-party identity provider. Identity pools enable customers to grant the users of their application access to components of the application hosted with AWS services, such as data stored in an S3 bucket.

Continue learning about Amazon Cognito by browsing the Amazon Cognito web page at aws.amazon.com/cognito/.

Identify resources for security support

Describe AWS Security Hub

AWS Security Hub is a security management service that enables customers to view the security status of their AWS environment and respond to and remediate security issues. Security Hub collects and aggregates data from multiple AWS accounts and security services, such as Amazon GuardDuty, Inspector, and Macie, as well as security products available from the AWS Partner Network (APN). When a customer enables Security Hub, the service automatically begins gathering data from the security services the customer has enabled and their integrated APN security products. Security Hub also begins automatically running checks to compare the customer's environment to AWS security best practice and industry standards. Security Hub analyzes the gathered data and the results of the automated checks to present the customer with findings showing potential security issues in their AWS environment. The customer can manually respond to and remediate issues from the findings or they can integrate Security Hub with Amazon EventBridge and configure actions to automatically remediate issues.

Continue learning about the AWS Security Hub by browsing the AWS Security Hub web page at aws.amazon.com/security-hub/.

Describe how AWS Professional Services can help improve security and compliance

AWS Professional Services is a team of AWS experts that customers can engage through the AWS Sales team to provide guidance on implementing their AWS Cloud solutions. AWS Professional Services offers specialty practices including a practice to provide guidance to customers on security, risk, and compliance through best practices, frameworks, tools, and services. AWS Professional Services has also created many frameworks customers can use to guide their transformational journey while adopting the AWS Cloud. One framework created by AWS Professional Services is the AWS Cloud Adoption Framework (CAF) consisting of six perspectives, or areas of focus. The Security perspective of the CAF includes recommendations for selecting and implementing security controls to protect an AWS environment and meet compliance obligations.

Continue learning about AWS Professional Services by browsing the AWS Professional Services web page at aws.amazon.com/professional-services/.

Describe how the AWS Partner Network can help improve security and compliance

The AWS Partner Network (APN) is a program that consists of tens of thousands of global partners that build AWS cloud-ready solutions and provide services for AWS customers. AWS has designated certain APN partners as AWS Security Competency Partners with a deep expertise and proven success providing customers with security solutions and services. With Security Competency Partners, customers can easily find and buy software solutions that fit their use case and are ready to launch in the AWS Cloud.

Continue learning about the AWS Security Competency Partners by browsing the AWS Security Competency Partners web page at aws.amazon.com/security/partner-solutions/.

Describe how AWS Trusted Advisor can improve security and compliance

AWS Trusted Advisor is a support console that provides AWS customers with checks and guidance to optimize their AWS infrastructure, increase security and performance, reduce overall costs, and monitor service usage and limits. To optimize the security and compliance of a customer's AWS environment, Trusted Advisor analyzes their AWS resources and compares them to AWS security best practices. Based on the results, Trusted Advisor makes recommendations to address vulnerabilities, enable AWS security features, and optimize permissions. With AWS Basic and Developer support plans, customers have access to six Trusted Advisor security checks: S3 Bucket Permissions, Security Groups - Specific Ports Unrestricted, IAM Use, MFA on Root Account, EBS Public Snapshots, and RDS Public Snapshots. Customers with an AWS Business or Enterprise support plan have access to all 17 security checks with Trusted Advisor

Continue learning about how AWS Trusted Advisor can improves security and compliance by reading the Trusted Advisor check reference, Security section of the AWS Support User Guide.

Describe how AWS Marketplace can help with security

The AWS Marketplace is a digital catalog of software, data, and services from AWS partners that customers can purchase to build solutions and run their business in the AWS Cloud. The Marketplace includes software purpose built for many use cases, such as data analytics, high performance compute, and security. The third-party security products available in the AWS Marketplace enable customers to deploy comprehensive security solutions to protect the components of their workloads and the data stored in their AWS environment. The Marketplace includes security products for the following use cases, application security, infrastructure security, identity management, endpoint security, WAF and edge security, next generation firewall, managed security services, cloud security posture management, and security information and event management (SIEM).

Continue learning about the third-party security products available in the AWS Marketplace by browsing the Security Solutions in AWS Marketplace web page at aws.amazon.com/marketplace/solutions/security/.

Find resources to learn about AWS Cloud security

Security Learning is a web page on the AWS website that provides information on services, tools, and best practices AWS offers to increase security in the AWS Cloud. The page provides links to resources, such as whitepapers, blogs, and training courses, customers can access to learn more about securing an AWS environment.

Continue learning about the resources available to gain AWS Cloud Security knowledge by browsing the Security Learning web page at aws.amazon.com/security/security-learning/.

Find resources to learn about AWS Cloud compliance

Compliance Resources is a web page on the AWS website that provides links to AWS Compliance Programs, frequently asked questions, information on the AWS shared responsibility model, and other resources dedicated to maintaining compliance in the AWS Cloud. The Compliance Resources - Amazon Web Services (AWS) web page on the AWS website provides links to documentation on compliance best practices, methods for verifying and achieving compliance, and training courses dedicated to security and compliance.

Continue learning about the resources available to gain AWS Cloud compliance knowledge by browsing the AWS Compliance web page at aws.amazon.com/compliance and the Compliance Resources web page at aws.amazon.com/compliance/resources/.

Billing and Pricing
Exam Domain

Compare and contrast the various pricing models for AWS

List the three fundamental drivers of cost with AWS

The three fundamental drivers of cost with AWS are compute, storage, and outbound data transfer. Outbound data transfer is classified as any data that travels out of the AWS Cloud to the Internet to reach its destination, such as files downloaded from an S3 bucket, data transferred across Regions or Availability Zones, and data transferred from the AWS Cloud to on-premises environments. Data transferred into the AWS Cloud or within Availability Zones generally does not incur charges.

Continue learning about the three fundamental drivers of cost with AWS by reading Understand the fundamentals of pricing in the Key principles section of the How AWS Pricing Works whitepaper.

Describe the EC2 On-Demand pricing model

The EC2 On-Demand pricing model enables customers to launch EC2 instances with pay-as-you-go pricing. With On-Demand pricing, customers only pay for the compute capacity they use measured in price per second with no long-term commitments or upfront payments. The On-Demand pricing model is ideal for businesses with changing business needs or flexible budgets and customers with short-term compute needs. AWS recommends On-Demand Instances for applications with short-term, irregular workloads that cannot be interrupted. Customers pay hourly or by the second for the use of on-demand EC2 instances. On-Demand Instances offer the greatest flexibility but typically cost more than similar instances with other pricing models.

Continue learning about the EC2 On-Demand pricing model by browsing the EC2 On-Demand Pricing web page at aws.amazon.com/ec2/pricing/on-demand/.

Describe the EC2 Reserved Instance pricing model

The EC2 Reserved Instance pricing model enables AWS customers to pay upfront for the EC2 instances they would like to use. Reserved Instances can be purchased for either one or three years and can save customers up to 72% when compared to similar On-Demand Instances. Customers using the consolidated billing feature of AWS Organizations can take advantage of the Reserved Instance hourly pricing discount for any instances launched with the same instance type and in the same Availability Zone as any Reserved Instance. Customers can choose between two classes of Reserviced Instances (RIs): Standard and Convertible. The primary differences between the two classes include Standard RIs provide a greater discount and Convertible RIs provide greater flexibility allowing customers to change the instance family, operating system, and payment option as long as the resulting RI is of equal or greater value. Reserved Instances are ideal for businesses with predictable business needs or fixed budgets and customers who want to ensure they have the compute capacity they need when they need it. The Reserved Instance pricing model is similar to EC2 Instance Savings Plans. The primary difference between Instance Savings Plans and Reserved Instances is customers commit to paying for Reserved Instances based on the instance type and configuration whereas customers commit to paying for Instance Savings Plans based on a specific amount of compute usage measured per hour. AWS recommends Savings Plans over Reserved Instances as Savings Plans offer more flexibility and enable customers to change their usage, instance type and configuration, and even the compute service they use as their needs change.

Continue learning about the EC2 Reserved Instance pricing model by browsing the Amazon EC2 Reserved Instance Pricing web page at aws.amazon.com/ec2/pricing/reserved-instances/pricing/.

Describe AWS Savings Plans

AWS Savings Plans is a pricing model that offers customers lower pricing for committing to a specific amount of usage and paying for the usage upfront, partially upfront, or monthly over the course of the commitment. Customers can purchase Savings Plans for a one or three-year period for certain compute and machine learning services. AWS offers three types of Savings Plans: Compute, EC2 Instance, and Amazon SageMaker. Compute Savings Plans apply to three different compute services: Amazon EC2, AWS Lambda, and AWS Fargate. With Compute Savings Plans, customers can migrate compute workloads between the three services without changing hourly pricing. EC2 Instance Savings Plans are similar to the EC2 Reserved Instance pricing model and offer savings up to 72% over similar On-Demand Instances. The primary difference between Instance Savings Plans and Reserved Instances is customers commit to paying for Reserved Instances based on the instance type and configuration whereas customers commit to paying for Instance Savings Plans based on a consistent amount of compute usage measured per hour. AWS recommends Savings Plans over Reserved Instances as Savings Plans offer more flexibility and enable customers to change their usage, instance type and configuration, and even the compute service they use as their needs change. Amazon SageMaker Savings Plans offer customers a flexible usage-based pricing model for machine learning capabilities. With the SageMaker Savings Plan, customers can save up to 64% by committing to pay for the machine learning capabilities they use.

Continue learning about AWS Savings Plans by browsing the AWS Savings Plans web page at aws.amazon.com/savingsplans/.

Describe EC2 On-Demand Capacity Reservations

EC2 On-Demand Capacity Reservation is an offering from AWS which enables customers to reserve compute capacity for On-Demand Instances. Capacity

Reservations ensure EC2 resources are available for customers when they need to launch more instances to meet increasing demand. When customers create a Capacity Reservation, they specify the Availability Zone to reserve capacity in, the number of instances to reserve, and the configuration of the instances. When customers launch an instance that matches the configuration in the specified Availability Zone, the instance will automatically use the Capacity Reservation. AWS begins billing for On-Demand Capacity Reservations as soon as they are created. However, Capacity Reservations require no one or three-year commitment. When customers no longer need the EC2 capacity reserved, they can cancel the Capacity Reservation at any time or schedule it to end automatically at a specific time. AWS immediately stops billing for the Capacity Reservation when it is manually cancelled or automatically ended.

Continue learning about EC2 On-Demand Capacity Reservations by reading the Instances, Instance purchasing options, On-Demand Capacity Reservations section of the Amazon Elastic Compute Cloud User Guide for Linux Instances.

Describe EC2 Dedicated Hosts

An EC2 Dedicated Host is a physical server fully dedicated to the use of one AWS customer to launch EC2 instances. With Dedicated Hosts, a customer is guaranteed exclusive use of the physical server and all hardware installed. By ensuring only the customer's workloads are deployed on the physical server, a Dedicated Host enables the customer to better meet security and compliance requirements. Dedicated Hosts are similar to Dedicated Instances. The primary difference is with Dedicated Hosts, customers have visibility into the sockets, cores, and host ID, and they have targeted instance placement with more control over how instances are placed on a physical server. With Dedicated Hosts, there is host and instance affinity, which means an instance can be consistently launched on the same physical server. Dedicated Hosts are ideal for bring your own license use cases enabling customers to use their existing per-socket, per-core, or per-VM software licenses, such as licenses for Windows Server, Microsoft SQL Server, SUSE, and Linux Enterprise Server.

Continue learning about EC2 Dedicated Hosts by browsing the Amazon EC2 Dedicated Hosts web page at aws.amazon.com/ec2/dedicated-hosts/.

Describe EC2 Dedicated Instances

Dedicated Instances are Amazon EC2 instances that run in a VPC on physical servers dedicated to one AWS customer. With Dedicated Instances, multiple instances from the same AWS account can run on the servers, but instances from other AWS accounts cannot. AWS customers can purchase EC2 Dedicated Instances using the On-Demand or Reserved Instance pricing model. Dedicated Instances are ideal for customers that wish to take advantage of the benefits of the AWS Cloud but require their resources and data to be isolated due to security and compliance regulations. Dedicated Instances are similar to Dedicated Hosts. The primary difference is with Dedicated Instances, customers do not have visibility into the sockets, cores, and host ID, and they do not have control over how instances are placed on a physical server. With Dedicated Instances, each instance may reside on a different server each time one is launched.

Continue learning about EC2 Dedicated Instances by browsing the Amazon EC2 Dedicated Instances web page at aws.amazon.com/ec2/pricing/dedicated-instances/.

Describe EC2 Spot Instances

Spot Instances are Amazon EC2 instances customers can purchase that utilize unused capacity in a pool of compute resources dedicated to EC2 in the AWS Cloud. Spot Instances provide AWS customers with up to a 90% discount compared to instances launched using the On-Demand pricing model. When customers request an EC2 Spot Instance, they choose all instance configurations and Availability Zones that are sufficient for their workloads. Then, they choose an interruption behavior: Hibernate, Stop, or Terminate. If the capacity is no longer available for the Spot Instance, the instance will hibernate, stop, or terminate based on the chosen interruption behavior. EC2 Spot Instances are ideal for stateless, fault-tolerant, and flexible applications and tasks such as data analysis, batch jobs, background processing, optional tasks, and test & development workloads. Spot Instances are a good option for customers who can be flexible about when their applications run and customers who have applications that can be interrupted.

Continue learning about EC2 Spot Instances by browsing the Amazon EC2 Spot Instances web page at aws.amazon.com/ec2/spot/.

Describe how compute cost is billed

Compute cost is billed differently for each compute service offered in the AWS Cloud. Generally, compute cost is billed based on several criteria, such as the Region where the cloud compute resource is launched, the operating system that runs on the resource if it requires one, the compute, memory, and networking capacity assigned to it, and the duration the resource is running. If On-Demand pricing is used, a customer is billed for the compute resource while it is up and running and not when it is in a pending, stopping, stopped, shutting down, or terminated state. If reservation pricing is used, a customer is billed a flat rate for the duration the compute resource is reserved.

Continue learning about how compute cost is billed by reading Billing and purchase options on the Amazon EC2 FAQs web page at aws.amazon.com/ec2/faqs/.

Describe how storage cost is billed

Storage cost is billed differently for each storage service offered in the AWS Cloud. Generally, storage cost is billed based on several criteria, such as the Region where the resource is launched, the storage type configured, the amount of storage used or reserved per GB, the number of snapshots or other features used, and the data transferred out of the AWS Cloud.

Continue learning about how storage cost is billed by reading Billing in the General S3 FAQs section on the Amazon Simple Storage Service FAQs web page at aws.amazon.com/s3/faqs/.

Describe how outbound data transfer is billed

Outbound data transfer is billed per GB based on the amount of data transferred out of an application or resource, such as an Amazon S3 bucket or RDS DB instance. Data transferred from an AWS resource to a resource outside of the AWS Cloud is typically more expensive than data transferred to another AWS resource in a different Region. There is typically no charge for inbound data transfer or data transferred between AWS resources within the same Region.

Continue learning about how outbound data transfer is billed by reading Understand the fundamentals of pricing in the Key principles section of the How AWS Pricing Works whitepaper.

Describe how Amazon VPC is billed

Creating and using a VPC is free. However, AWS customers are billed for the resources that are launched in a VPC, such as EC2 instances and S3 buckets. Customers are also billed for resources and VPC features that provide connectivity between a VPC and their on-premises environment or the Internet, such as VPN connections and NAT gateways.

Continue learning about how Amazon VPC is billed by browsing the Amazon VPC pricing web page at aws.amazon.com/vpc/pricing/.

Describe how Amazon EC2 is billed

AWS offers Amazon EC2 instance types optimized to fit many different use cases. Each instance type customers can choose from has a specific number of vCPU cores, memory, storage type, and networking capacity. Instance types with greater capacity are billed at a higher hourly rate than those with lower capacity. AWS also offers multiple operating systems customers can choose from for their EC2 instances. Operating system licensing is included with the price of the instance, and Windows instances are generally billed at a higher rate than Linux instances. AWS offers many ways to pay for EC2 instances, including On-Demand Instances, Reserved Instances,

EC2 Savings Plans, Spot Instances, and Dedicated Hosts. With On-Demand Instances, customers are billed each month for the instance while it is up and running. On-Demand Instances are the most flexible option enabling customers to add or remove capacity as needed without committing to paying for the instance beyond the time it is in use. Spot Instances allow customers to enter a maximum bid for a Spot Instance that will utilize surplus EC2 capacity in the AWS Cloud. The price of Spot Instances changes with supply and demand of unused EC2 capacity. If the current price of a Spot Instance is greater than the customer's maximum bid, the Spot Instance will hibernate, stop, or terminate depending on the interruption behavior chosen by the customer when the instance was launched. Spot Instances save AWS customers up to 90% on compute cost compared to On-Demand Instances. With Reserved Instances and instances with a Savings Plan, customers commit to purchasing an EC2 instance for one or three years. Reserved Instances and Savings Plan instances are billed for the entire duration of the reservation at a reduced hourly rate up to 72% less than On-Demand Instances. A Dedicated Host is a physical server allocated to one AWS customer to launch EC2 instances. Dedicated Hosts can be billed On-Demand, as a Reservation, or as part of a Savings Plan. The price of a Dedicated Host depends on the instance configuration and the Region in which it is launched. Dedicated hosts are billed per second while the instance is allocated to the customer account.

Continue learning about how Amazon EC2 is billed by reading the Pricing details for individual services, Amazon Elastic Compute Cloud (Amazon EC2) section of the How AWS Pricing Works whitepaper.

Describe how Amazon S3 is billed

The pricing of Amazon S3 storage may change depending on the Region where the S3 bucket resides. However, the considerations AWS takes into account when billing for S3 storage are the same in each Region and include the storage class, storage used, requests and data retrievals, outbound data transfer, and management features and replication. Each object stored in an S3 bucket has a storage class associated with it. The storage class determines the level of performance a customer should expect when the object is accessed. Objects that are stored with a higher performing storage class are billed higher than those stored with lower performing classes. AWS customers are not billed when they create an S3 bucket. Billing only begins when objects are uploaded, copied, or moved to the bucket. For the S3 Standard and S3 Intelligent - Tiering storage classes, AWS uses a tiered pricing model. For the first 50 TB stored in a month, AWS bills a certain rate per GB. For the next 450 TB, AWS bills a lower rate per GB. For over 500 TB stored, AWS bills the lowest rate per GB. AWS bills for each HTTP or REST request to retrieve or modify data in an S3 bucket. For each request to modify data, such as POST, COPY, PUT, and LIST, AWS bills a higher rate than each request to retrieve data, such as GET and SELECT. AWS bills a certain rate per GB to transfer data from an S3 bucket to the Internet or to an AWS resource in a different Region. Data transfer to AWS resources in the same Region are not billed. However, if the data is transferred programmatically, each HTTP or REST request will be billed based on the Amazon S3 request billing rate. Many Amazon S3 storage management features are billable when they are enabled on a bucket, such as replication, S3 inventory, analytics, and object tagging.

Continue learning about how Amazon S3 is billed by reading the Pricing details for individual services, Amazon Simple Storage Service (Amazon S3) section of the How AWS Pricing Works whitepaper.

Describe how Amazon EBS is billed

There are three factors AWS takes into consideration when billing for Amazon EBS resources: volumes, snapshots, and outbound data transfer. When customers provision an EBS volume, they are billed per GB for the space provisioned. If a customer creates a 1 TB volume, they will be billed monthly for 1 TB until the volume is deleted. When customers create an EBS volume, they choose the volume type which determines the type of storage media the data will be stored on: SSD or HDD. SSD-backed volumes are billed at a higher price per GB than HDD-backed volumes. AWS also bills customers per month for EBS snapshots based on the space consumed by the data in the snapshots. AWS considers any data transferred out of an instance that uses an EBS volume to be outbound data transfer and billable per GB transferred. EBS snapshots copied from one AWS Region to another Region are also considered outbound data transfer and are billable.

Continue learning about how Amazon EBS is billed by reading the Pricing details for individual services, Amazon Elastic Block Store (Amazon EBS) section of the How AWS Pricing Works whitepaper.

Describe how Amazon RDS is billed

Billing for Amazon RDS includes all three fundamental drivers of cost: compute, storage, and outbound data transfer. Compute time is billed differently for each database engine RDS offers. For example, DB instances launched with Amazon RDS for Microsoft SQL are priced higher than equivalent DB instances launched with Amazon RDS for MySQL. RDS DB instances can be launched with an On-Demand pricing model or a Reserved Instance pricing model. With On-Demand Instances, AWS bills customers based on an hourly rate only while the DB instance is up and running. With Reserved Instances, customers pay a flat rate each month for the DB instance for the entire term of the instance reservation. When a DB instance is launched, customers select a class type determining the compute, memory, and network capacity of the instance. The greater the capacity, the higher rate AWS bills for the instance. Storage for an RDS DB instance is billed per GB of storage consumed. Storage is also billed based on the number of input and output (I/O) requests to access the stored data. Requests are billed in terms of I/O per second for Provisioned IOPS (SSD) Storage and per million I/O requests for Magnetic Storage. With General Purpose (SSD) Storage, AWS does not bill for I/O requests. Data transferred into a DB instance is not billable. However, AWS bills per GB of data transferred out to the Internet based on a tiered pricing model. AWS bills a certain price per GB for the first 10 TB of data transferred out per month and bills increasingly lower for the next 40 TB, the next 100 TB, and greater than 150 TB per month. Data transferred across AWS Regions is considered outbound data transfer and is billed per GB of data transferred.

Continue learning about how Amazon RDS is billed by reading the Pricing details for individual services, Amazon RDS section of the How AWS Pricing Works whitepaper.

Describe how Amazon CloudFront is billed

Amazon CloudFront is billed based on actual usage in four areas: data transfer out, HTTP/HTTPS requests, invalidation requests, and field level encryption requests. Data transferred out of CloudFront to the Internet is billed per GB and follows a tiered pricing model each month based on the amount of data that is transferred. Data transferred out of CloudFront to an AWS resource in a different Region is billed based on a single per GB rate no matter how much data is transferred each month. The price per GB of data transferred out varies from Region to Region and is dependent on where the Edge Location is that serves the content to the end user. AWS bills a certain amount for each HTTP request to access objects in a CloudFront distribution. Like data transfer out, the price for each request depends on where the Edge Location is that serves content to the end user. HTTPS requests to access objects are billed at a higher rate than HTTP requests. When customers no longer want content available in an Edge Location, they can invalidate a file or a path to multiple files to remove the content from the Edge Location. AWS allows a certain number of invalidation requests for free each month and charges for each request after the free requests are used up. Field level encryption is an option offered with CloudFront to encrypt data in specific fields of HTTPS requests. Field level encryption requests are billed based on the number of HTTPS requests where the additional encryption is used.

Continue learning about how Amazon CloudFront is billed by reading the Pricing details for individual services, Amazon CloudFront section of the How AWS Pricing Works whitepaper.

Recognize the various account structures in relation to AWS billing and pricing

Describe the AWS Free Tier

The AWS Free Tier provides customers access to various AWS services and resources for free to gain hands-on experience, test workloads, and learn more about how AWS can benefit them and their business. The Free Tier is automatically included with all AWS accounts and provides three different types of free offerings: trials, 12-months free, and always free. Trials provide short-term access to various AWS services and start from the date the service is activated. 12-months free offerings provide access to various AWS services for 12 months starting from the time the AWS account is created. Always free offerings do not expire and provide customers with a certain amount of usage for free before they are billed for consuming AWS resources. Each offer in the Free Tier has a predetermined limit for the amount of usage that is free. Once the limit is reached, customers will be billed for any further consumption of any provisioned AWS resources. In order to avoid incurring charges once the limit is reached, AWS recommends configuring AWS Free Tier usage alerts with AWS Budgets.

Continue learning about the AWS Free Tier by browsing the AWS Free Tier web page at aws.amazon.com/free/.

Describe AWS Organizations

AWS Organizations is an account management service enabling customers to centrally manage and govern AWS accounts. With Organizations, an administrator can create an organization and add member accounts by either creating new accounts or inviting existing AWS accounts to join the organization. The account that creates an organization is called the management account, and all other accounts in the organization are called member accounts. Managing member accounts in an organization enables administrators to consolidate billing and pay for charges incurred by all member accounts, attach policies to centrally manage control over AWS services and API actions, attach policies to standardize tags across accounts, and govern budgetary, security, and compliance needs across the organization. Within an organization, an administrator can create organizational units (OUs) to group member accounts into a hierarchical structure. Grouping member accounts into OUs enables an administrator to view and manage policies and billing on multiple levels, including for the entire organization, for a single OU, or for a single member account. AWS Organizations can integrate with other AWS services, such as AWS Backup to configure policies for backing up data across the organization and AWS IAM to control access and authorization for users and roles in member accounts. AWS does not charge for the use of AWS Organizations. The service and features are free to use for all customers.

Continue learning about AWS Organizations by browsing the AWS Organizations web page at aws.amazon.com/organizations/.

Describe consolidating billing for AWS Organizations

An account is the entity AWS bills for all charges incurred from the usage of AWS resources provisioned in the account. Consolidated billing is a feature of AWS Organizations that combines the charges incurred by all accounts in the organization into a single view accessible in the AWS Billing console for the management account. With consolidated billing, member accounts are not billed individually. Instead, the management account is billed for all charges incurred by the accounts in the organization. Consolidated billing enables customers to take advantage of volume discounts, Reserved Instance discounts, and Savings Plans by using a single payment method to pay for the AWS resources consumed by all accounts in an organization.

Continue learning about consolidated billing by reading the Consolidated billing for AWS Organizations section in the AWS Billing User Guide.

Describe cost allocation tags

Tags are metadata labels that can be applied to AWS resources to identify and organize resources for billing and administration purposes. Tags can be applied to a resource when the resource is created or they can be applied to existing resources individually or as a group using Tag Editor. Cost allocation tags are a type of tag that can be applied to resources to categorize and track the costs of resource usage on monthly cost allocation reports. There are two types of cost allocation tags: AWS generated tags and user-defined tags. AWS generated cost allocation tags must be enabled for an account by activating the createdBy tag in the AWS Billing console for the account. When the createdBy tag is activated for an account, AWS begins applying the tag to any new resource created to track who created the resource. As the resource is used, AWS records the resource usage costs and the name of the IAM user that created the resource on the customer's cost allocation report. User-defined cost allocation tags can be created by customers and applied to any resources they create and own. After user-defined cost allocation tags are applied to a resource, cost allocation tracking must be activated in the AWS Billing console for the account to begin tracking cost on the cost allocation report for each resource that has a cost allocation tag applied.

Continue learning about cost allocation tags by reading the Using AWS cost allocation tags section of the AWS Billing User Guide.

List common billing account structures for multi-account AWS environments

In multi-account AWS environments, administrators of AWS Organizations commonly use four different AWS billing account structures: Business Unit, Environment Lifecycle, Project-Based, and Hybrid. The account structures help administrators group member accounts into organizational units to create a hierarchical structure and strategically manage billing of all accounts in an organization.

Continue learning about AWS billing account structures by reading the AWS Account Structures section of the AWS Multiple Account Billing Strategy whitepaper.

Describe the AWS Business Unit account structure

The AWS Business Unit (BU) account structure works well for organizations in which each business unit is responsible for its own IT administration, operations, and costs. With the BU account structure, an administrator creates an organizational unit (OU) for each business unit, such as sales, retail, and finance. The administrator then creates or moves each member account into the appropriate OU representing their business unit. This enables the administrator to view the charges incurred by each business unit and take any action deemed fit, such as internally billing each business unit for its usage.

Continue learning about the AWS Business Unit account structure by reading the Business Unit (BU) Account Structure section of the AWS Multiple Account Billing Strategy whitepaper.

Describe the AWS Environment Lifecycle account structure

The AWS Environment Lifecycle account structure works well for organizations who want to align billing with their application deployment lifecycle. With this account structure, an administrator creates an organizational unit (OU) for each environment used while developing an application, such as development, test, staging, and production. The administrator creates or moves each member account into the OU representing the environment in which they work. This enables the administrator to view the charges incurred in each environment and determine in which environments the organization is making the largest investment while developing, testing, and hosting applications.

Continue learning about the AWS Environment Lifecycle account structure by reading the Environment Lifecycle Account Structure section of the AWS Multiple Account Billing Strategy whitepaper.

Describe the AWS Project-Based account structure

The AWS Project-Based account structure works well for organizations who want to align billing with projects being worked on in the business. With this account structure, an administrator creates an organizational unit (OU) for each project. The administrator creates or moves each project member account into the OU representing the project. This enables the administrator to view the charges incurred for each project and determine in which projects the organization is making the largest investment.

Continue learning about the AWS Project-Based account structure by reading the Project-Based Account Structure section of the AWS Multiple Account Billing Strategy whitepaper.

Describe Hybrid AWS account structures

In larger organizations, it may be beneficial to group accounts by more than one dimension. In such cases, a Hybrid AWS account structure can be used in which an administrator creates a separate organization for each appropriate grouping of organizational units. Then, the administrator creates organizational units for the appropriate grouping of member accounts. One example of a Hybrid AWS account structure is an administrator that wishes to group member accounts into projects and then group projects into business units. The administrator would create an organization for each business unit. Then, in each organization, the administrator would create an organizational unit for each project being work on in the business unit. Finally, in each project organizational unit, the administrator would create or move each member account that is working on the project. This would allow the administrator to view the charges incurred for each member account, project, and business unit accordingly.

Continue learning about Hybrid AWS account structures by reading the Hybrid AWS Account Structures section of the AWS Multiple Account Billing Strategy whitepaper.

Identify resources available for billing support

Describe the AWS Billing console

AWS Billing and Cost Management is a cloud financial management service that provides customers with features and tools to manage ongoing payments and optimize future costs of resources in their AWS environment. There are two consoles customers can use with the AWS Billing and Cost Management service: AWS Cost Management console and AWS Billing console. The Billing console includes features and tools to help customers gather cost and usage information, analyze cost drivers and usage trends, and budget their spending. AWS Cost Categories is a feature of the Billing console customers can use to create rules to organize costs into categories that can be used in multiple other features of the AWS Billing and Cost Management consoles, such as Cost Explorer and AWS Cost and Usage Reports. AWS Credits is another feature of the console that automatically applies any AWS promotional credits accrued by eligible services to customers AWS bill. Other features of the Billing console include AWS Cost Allocation Tags, AWS Cost and Usage Reports, AWS Consolidated Billing, AWS Purchase Order Management, and the AWS Free Tier. The AWS Billing console is closely integrated with the AWS Cost Management console and they are presented to customers together in one user interface. Customers commonly use both consoles together to get a comprehensive view of their usage and take a holistic approach to managing cost. Customers can use the Cost Management console to optimize future costs and the Billing console to manage ongoing payments.

Continue learning about the AWS Billing console by reading the What is AWS Billing? section of the AWS Billing User Guide.

Describe the AWS Billing console dashboard

The AWS Billing console dashboard is the default view when customers access the Billing console. The dashboard includes graphs and other visualizations that provide customers with a general, high-level view of their AWS cost and spending. The dashboard enables customers to compare current and forecasted costs to the prior billing period, identify the highest month-to-date cost service, account, and Region, and view cost trends of the top services and the account for the most recent three to six billing periods. The following sections are available and visible by default in the dashboard, AWS summary, Highest cost and usage details, Cost trend of top five services, and Account cost trend. Customers can customize their dashboard by moving sections to change the layout and by removing sections from the view.

Continue learning about the AWS Billing console dashboard by reading the Using the AWS Billing console dashboard section of the AWS Billing User Guide.

Describe AWS Cost and Usage Reports

AWS Cost and Usage Reports (CUR) is a feature of AWS Billing enabling customers to gain an in-depth view of the cost and usage of resources in their AWS environment. Out of all AWS Billing and Cost Management features, CUR provides customers with the most detailed and comprehensive view of their AWS cost and billing. Customers can create Cost and Usage Reports in the AWS Billing console. When creating a report, customers configure the following settings: the S3 bucket where they want AWS to store the generated CUR files, the time granularity they want the report to break down costs by (hour, day, or month), report versioning to determine if AWS should create a new CUR file or overwrite the existing file each time a report is generated, and the option to include Resource IDs in the reports and create individual line items for each resource in the CUR file. CUR files generated by Cost and Usage Reports are in CSV file format and contain account identifiers, invoice and bill information, usage amount and unit, rates and cost, product attributes, pricing attributes, and reservation identifiers and related details for Reserved Instances. To view CUR files and analyze their cost and usage, customers can use spreadsheet software, like Microsoft Excel or Apache OpenOffice Calc, or any application that supports CSV files. Alternately, customers can configure report data integrations when creating a report in order to use Amazon Athena, RedShift, or QuickSight for in-depth analysis of cost and usage data in the AWS Cloud. Customers commonly use AWS Cost and Usage Reports to enable chargeback for departments or teams in the organization. Customers also commonly use CUR to analyze spikes and trends in resource cost and usage to take action and optimize cost in their AWS environment.

Continue learning about AWS Cost and Usage Reports by browsing the AWS Cost and Usage Reports web page at aws.amazon.com/aws-cost-management/aws-cost-and-usage-reporting/.

Describe the AWS Cost Management console

AWS Billing and Cost Management is a cloud financial management service that provides customers with features and tools to manage ongoing payments and optimize future costs of resources in their AWS environment. There are two consoles customers can use with the AWS Billing and Cost Management service: AWS Cost Management console and AWS Billing console. The Cost Management console includes features and tools to help customers budget and forecast costs and optimize pricing to reduce their overall AWS bill. Rightsizing recommendations is a feature of the Cost Management console which reviews EC2 usage and makes recommendations to help customers align their instance capacity with their workload demand. AWS Cost Anomaly Detection is another feature of the console that helps customers identify factors driving increased cost by using machine learning to continuously monitor usage and cost and detect unusual spends. Other features of the Cost Management console include AWS Cost Explorer, AWS Budgets, and Savings Plans. The AWS Cost Management console is closely integrated with the AWS Billing console and they are presented to customers together in one user interface. Customers commonly use both consoles together to get a comprehensive view of their usage and take a holistic approach to managing cost. Customers can use the Billing console to manage ongoing payments and the Cost Management console to optimize future costs.

Continue learning about the AWS Cost Management console by reading the What is AWS Cost Management? section of the AWS Cost Management User Guide.

Describe AWS Cost Explorer

AWS Cost Explorer is a tool customers can enable in the AWS Cost Management to view and analyze their AWS costs and usage. After Cost Explorer is enabled, AWS gathers the customer's cost for the current month and last 12 months and makes it available in Cost Explorer within 24 hours. AWS also calculates forecasted cost for the next 12 months and makes it available within a few days after the current and past cost is available. Customers can view charts and reports on their cost and usage in the Cost Explorer user interface for free or they can programmatically access cost and usage data using the Cost Explorer API for a small charge per API request. When customers launch the Cost Explorer user interface, the Cost dashboard is displayed showing the estimated costs for the month to date, the forecasted costs for the month, a graph of the daily costs, the five top cost trends, and a list of reports the customer recently viewed. In Cost Explorer, customers have access to default reports that show their resource usage and the cost incurred for the past 6 months. Customers can use filters, groups, and other options in the default reports to view their cost and usage in a custom report. Then, the customers can save the report to view later in their list of saved reports. Cost Explorer includes RI reports customers can access to view and analyze the cost and usage of their Reserved Instances. Customers can also access RI recommendations for the Reserved Instances they can purchase to optimize cost based on historical cost and usage.

Continue learning about AWS Cost Explorer by browsing the AWS Cost Explorer web page at aws.amazon.com/aws-cost-management/aws-cost-explorer/.

Describe AWS Budgets

AWS Budgets is a feature of AWS Cost Management enabling customers to monitor actual and forecasted cost and usage of resources in their AWS environment. Customers can create budgets in the Cost Management console and configure thresholds for the cost, usage, and coverage of their AWS resources. A budget can be configured to alert the customer via email or SNS notification when a threshold is reached enabling the customer to take action when their cost or usage exceeds their expectations or when their resources are under-utilized. Customers can also set up custom actions to automatically apply an IAM policy or attach a service control policy to resources when cost or usage reaches the threshold configured in a budget. AWS Budgets integrates with Cost Explorer to display a graph enabling customers to view and analyze their incurred cost and usage in the Cost Explorer user interface. There are four types of budgets customers can create in the Cost Management console: cost, usage, reservation, and Savings Plans. A cost budget enables customers to plan, monitor, and respond to how much they spend on AWS services ensuring they don't go above their expected cost. A usage budget enables them to plan, monitor, and respond to how much of one or more services they are using in their AWS environment. With reservation budgets, customers can configure thresholds and receive alerts when either the utilization or coverage of their Reserved Instances (RIs) drop below the threshold. Reservation budgets help customers monitor their RIs ensuring the instances are not under-utilized and they are receiving the best return on their upfront investment. Savings Plans budgets serve the same purpose and are configured in the same manner as reservation budgets and help customers ensure their Savings Plans are utilized efficiently.

Continue learning about AWS Budgets by browsing the AWS Budgets web page at aws.amazon.com/aws-cost-management/aws-budgets/.

Describe Amazon CloudWatch billing alarms

An alarm is a feature of Amazon CloudWatch customers can configure to monitor metrics of their AWS resources and automatically take an action when a specified condition is met or an anomaly is detected. Common actions customers configure alarms to perform when triggered include notifying people using Amazon SNS topics, stopping or terminating EC2 instances, and scaling Auto Scaling groups up or down. Common metrics customers monitor with CloudWatch alerts include CPU usage, load balancer latency, storage throughput, and AWS charges. Customers can enable and configure billing alarms to monitor the charges in their AWS environment and take an action when their estimated charges reach a specified threshold. CloudWatch billing alarms allow customers to monitor their estimated charges and proactively optimize the cost of the AWS environment.

Continue learning about Amazon CloudWatch billing alarms by reading the Alarms, Creating a billing alarm section of the Amazon CloudWatch User Guide.

Describe how AWS Trusted Advisor helps reduce overall cost

AWS Trusted Advisor is a support console that provides customers with best practice checks and guidance to optimize their AWS infrastructure, increase security and performance, reduce overall costs, and monitor service usage and limits. Trusted Advisor analyzes a customer's AWS environment and compares it to AWS cost optimization best practices. Based on the comparison, Trusted Advisor makes recommendations to save the customer money on AWS resources by eliminating unused and idle resources or by making commitments to reserved capacity. With an AWS Basic Support or Developer Support plan, customers do not have access to any Trusted Advisor cost optimization checks. Customers with an AWS Business Support, Enterprise On-Ramp Support, or Enterprise Support plan have access to all 20 cost optimization checks.

Continue learning about the AWS Trusted Advisor cost optimization checks by reading the AWS Trusted Advisor, Trusted Advisor check reference, Cost optimization section of the AWS Support User Guide.

Describe how the Amazon Partner Network can help with resource and cost optimization

The Amazon Partner Network (APN) is global community of individuals and organizations that Amazon has reviewed to ensure they have AWS expertise and can offer software, data, and services that will help customers build solutions and run their business in the AWS Cloud. Partners in the APN can become a Competency partner if they have demonstrated AWS technical expertise and proven customer success in specialized areas, such as Machine Learning, Data and Analytics, and Cloud Management Tools. The AWS Cloud Management Tools Competency includes two categories: Cloud Governance and Resource and Cost Optimization. Customers can purchase partner solutions offered in the Resource and Cost Optimization Competency category to help them gain visibility into their AWS cost and usage and provide recommendations on optimizing their resources and maximizing their investment in the AWS Cloud.

Continue learning about the Cloud Management Tools Competency and Resource and Cost Optimization category by browsing the AWS Cloud Management Tools Competency Partners web page at aws.amazon.com/products/management-tools/partner-solutions/.

Describe how AWS Marketplace can help with cloud cost management

The AWS Marketplace is a digital catalog of software, data, and services from AWS partners that customers can purchase to build solutions and run their business in the AWS Cloud. In the AWS Marketplace, customers will find tools for cloud cost management that will help them gain visibility into their AWS cost ensuring they avoid unintentional high charges and have full control over their AWS spend. Customers commonly purchase cloud cost management tools in the Marketplace to help them reduce waste, optimize their resources for efficiency, and provide dashboards and reports to inform them of their AWS resource cost and usage.

Continue learning about the cloud cost management tools available in the AWS Marketplace by browsing the Cloud Cost Management web page at aws.amazon.com/marketplace/solutions/business-applications/cloud-cost-management/.

Describe the AWS Pricing Calculator

The AWS Pricing Calculator is a public online tool anybody can use to estimate the cost of services and solutions in the AWS Cloud. With the Pricing Calculator, new and existing customers select the service they will use and the configuration of the resources they will provision with the service. Then, the Pricing Calculator shows the estimated monthly cost of the configured resources. If the customer wants to view the estimated cost for an entire solution, they click the "Add to my estimate" button, and continue adding additional services until all services in the solution are added to their estimate. Once all services and configurations have been added to the customer's estimate, the customer can view the upfront and monthly cost of each service individually and the upfront cost, monthly cost, and total 12-month cost of the entire solution.

Continue learning about the AWS Pricing Calculator by reading the What is AWS Pricing Calculator? section of the AWS Pricing Calculator User Guide.

Describe the AWS Price List API

The AWS Price List API enables customers to programmatically access prices for AWS services. Customers commonly use the Price List API to gather AWS service pricing data using budgeting, forecasting, and analytics tools to evaluate the feasibility and cost-effectiveness of moving their on-premises workloads to the AWS Cloud. Customers can also use the Price List API to be notified when the pricing for AWS services changes by subscribing to AWS Price List API topics with Amazon SNS. AWS offers two Price List APIs: AWS Price List Bulk API and AWS Price List Query API. The bulk API enables customers to gather the prices of all AWS services in bulk by using a URL to download a JSON or CSV file with current and historical pricing for all AWS Services. The query API enables customers to perform fine-grained queries to return specific pricing information about AWS services and products ensuring customers and their tools receive only the information they need. The query API is ideal for mobile and browser-based applications that are not capable of parsing large and complex JSON and CSV files. However, query API does not support Savings Plans pricing. Customers paying for AWS resources using Savings Plans must use the bulk API to programmatically access pricing for AWS services.

Continue learning about the AWS Price List API by reading the Monitoring your usage and costs, Using the AWS Price List API, Using the query API section and the Monitoring your usage and costs, Using the AWS Price List API, Using the bulk API section of the AWS Billing User Guide.

Find pricing for AWS services manually

AWS hosts a web page on aws.amazon.com for each AWS service. On the web page for each service, there is a pricing tab that includes all relevant pricing information for the service, including purchasing options, pricing models, and pricing for any features that will incur a cost. You can find the most up-to-date pricing for each AWS service manually by visiting the web page of the service and selecting the Pricing tab. Alternately, you can find pricing for AWS services manually by using the Services Pricing section of the AWS Pricing web page which includes links to the Pricing tab of each AWS service.

Continue learning how to manually find pricing for AWS services by browsing the Pricing for AWS products section of the AWS Pricing web page at aws.amazon.com/pricing/.

Describe the AWS Concierge Support Team

Customers with AWS Enterprise On-Ramp Support and Enterprise Support plans have access to the AWS Concierge Support Team. The Concierge Support Team is a team of AWS billing and account experts that assists Enterprise customers with billing and account questions. Concierge Support also helps customers implement billing and account best practices to optimize cost in their AWS environments.

Continue learning about the AWS Concierge Support Team by reading the Common AWS Concierge customer questions on the AWS Premium Support FAQs web page at aws.amazon.com/premiumsupport/faqs/.

Open an account and billing support case

Customers can create an account and billing support case using the AWS Support Center in the AWS Management Console. After logging in to the Console, a customer selects Support in the upper right corner, selects Support Center, and selects Create case. Next, the customer must select the Account and billing support option, fill in the required fields in the form, choose the contact method, and select Submit. After the case is submitted, an AWS Support representative will contact the customer within 24 hours.

Continue learning about how to open an account and billing support case by reading Contacting AWS Support in the Getting help section of the AWS Billing User Guide.

AWS CLF-C01 Practice Test

The practice test is designed to help you prepare for the AWS Certified Cloud Practitioner CLF-C01 exam. The test includes 50 questions which is the same number of questions AWS scores on the actual exam. The questions are modeled after those that you will see on the exam, including similar phrasing and format, to ensure you know what to expect when you take the exam.

All four exam domains and capabilities are covered in the practice test using the same distribution as the actual exam: 26% Cloud Concepts, 33% Technology, 25% Compliance & Security, and 16% Billing & Pricing. Use the answer key immediately following the practice test to score your test, and see how prepared you are for the CLF-C01 exam.

For more practice tests, visit our website at informedreadiness.com, or purchase the practice tests book from the author on Amazon, Apple Books, Barnes & Noble, or any online store where you purchase your books.

1. Which of the following cloud computing models provides customers with the most control over the compute, storage, and networking resources delivered by a cloud provider?
   A. Application-as-a-Service (AaaS)
   B. Infrastructure-as-a-Service (IaaS)
   C. Platform-as-a-Service (PaaS)
   D. Software-as-a-Service (SaaS)

2. Which of the following statements best describes the deployment models offered by AWS?
   A. The On-premises (private cloud) deployment model allows customers to access AWS resources over the internet.
   B. The Cloud (public cloud) deployment model allows customers to access AWS resources over the internet.
   C. The Hybrid cloud deployment model allows customers to access AWS resources solely over the internet.
   D. The Cloud (public Cloud) deployment model allows customers to build a cloud environment within their own data centers.

3. Which AWS service can help achieve fault tolerance for applications by automatically distributing incoming traffic across multiple instances?
   A. Amazon Simple Notification Service (SNS)
   B. Amazon Elastic Compute Cloud (EC2)
   C. Amazon Elastic Load Balancing (ELB)
   D. AWS Auto Scaling

4. Which of the following statements best describes the concept of elasticity in AWS?
   A. Elasticity refers to the ability of an AWS service to scale up or down automatically in response to changes in demand or traffic.
   B. Elasticity refers to the ability of an AWS service to provide unlimited resources to users, regardless of their usage patterns.

C. Elasticity refers to the ability of an AWS service to provide high availability and fault tolerance through the use of multiple redundant resources.

D. Elasticity refers to the ability of an AWS service to provide low latency and high throughput to users, regardless of their location.

5. Which AWS service enables customers to trade fixed expense for variable expense by paying only for the compute resources they use instead of making upfront capital investments in hardware and infrastructure?
   A. Amazon S3
   B. Amazon EC2
   C. AWS Elastic Beanstalk
   D. Amazon Glacier

6. Which of the following statements is true about AWS tiered pricing?
   A. AWS tiered pricing provides a fixed cost per hour for using AWS services, regardless of the usage level.
   B. AWS tiered pricing provides a volume-based pricing model, where customers pay a fixed cost per unit of usage.
   C. AWS tiered pricing provides a customized pricing model, where customers can negotiate their own rates with AWS.
   D. AWS tiered pricing provides discounts based on the amount of usage, with lower rates for higher usage.

7. Which of the following statements best describes how AWS fully managed services help customers save on costs?
   A. AWS fully managed services offer upfront pricing, allowing customers to easily budget for their infrastructure costs.
   B. AWS manages all underlying operating systems and software ensuring operations personnel are not required to patch and maintain systems.
   C. Customers manage and maintain the underlying infrastructure and software ensuring they can configure software to their exact specifications.
   D. AWS fully managed services offer more complex solutions resulting in greater return on investment.

8. Which AWS service helps customers stop guessing capacity and provision the exact amount of resources needed to support their applications?
   A. Amazon CloudFront
   B. Amazon Elastic Compute Cloud (EC2)
   C. AWS Auto Scaling
   D. AWS Lambda

9. Which of the following statements best describes the AWS Well-Architected Framework?
   A. It is a set of guidelines for building secure, high-performance, resilient, cost optimized, and sustainable infrastructure in the AWS Cloud.
   B. It is a collection of pre-built architectures that can be deployed in the AWS Cloud to speed up the development process.
   C. It is a tool that helps you monitor and optimize the cost of your AWS infrastructure.
   D. It is a certification program that validates your expertise in designing and deploying applications on the AWS platform.

10. A customer wants to decouple components of a workload in the AWS Cloud. Which AWS services will enable this? (Select two)
    A. Amazon RDS
    B. Amazon API Gateway
    C. Amazon SQS
    D. Amazon S3

11. Which pillar of the AWS Well-Architected Framework focuses on ensuring that workloads are run efficiently and that organizations can continuously improve their processes and procedures?
    A. Operational Excellence
    B. Performance Efficiency
    C. Reliability
    D. Security

12. Which of the following statements best describes the Reliability pillar of the AWS Well-Architected Framework?
    A. It is a set of principles for achieving highly available and fault-tolerant architectures that can recover from failures in the AWS Cloud.
    B. It is a set of practices for running and monitoring your systems to deliver business value and continuously improve your processes in the AWS Cloud.
    C. It is a set of best practices for designing and operating secure and compliant IT systems in the AWS Cloud.
    D. It is a set of guidelines for designing and operating sustainable and efficient IT systems that minimize the environmental impact of your workloads.

13. A customer wants to think parallel in the AWS Cloud by providing shared access to a file system and improving performance. Which AWS service will enable this?
    A. Amazon S3
    B. Amazon EBS
    C. Amazon RDS
    D. Amazon EFS

14. Which of the following AWS management tools includes a set of programming libraries in various programming languages used to interact with AWS services?
    A. AWS SDKs
    B. AWS Management Console
    C. AWS CLIs
    D. Amazon API Gateway

15. Which of the following statements are true regarding AWS Transit Gateway? (Select two)
    A. AWS Transit Gateway is enables customers to connect their Amazon VPCs and on-premises networks through a single gateway.
    B. AWS Transit Gateway is limited to connecting a maximum of two VPCs.
    C. AWS Transit Gateway can only be used to connect VPCs in the AWS Cloud.
    D. AWS Transit Gateway supports both IPv4 and IPv6 traffic.

16. Which AWS service can customers use to implement hybrid cloud in the AWS Cloud and bypass the public internet to establish a private connection to AWS?
    A. Amazon Redshift
    B. Amazon VPN
    C. AWS Direct Connect
    D. Amazon CloudFront

17. A customer wants to implement Kubernetes to run containerized applications in the AWS Cloud? Which AWS service will enable this?
    A. Amazon S3
    B. Amazon EC2
    C. Amazon ECS
    D. Amazon EKS

18. Which of the following statements best describes the purpose of AWS Regions?
    A. AWS Regions provide low-latency connectivity between AWS services.
    B. AWS Regions are used to manage access control and security for AWS resources.
    C. AWS Regions are used to specify the geographic location of AWS resources.
    D. AWS Regions are used to reduce the cost of running AWS resources.

19. Which of the following statements best describes the relationship between AWS Availability Zones and reliability?
    A. AWS Availability Zones are the only way to achieve high reliability for AWS resources.
    B. AWS Availability Zones provide an additional layer of reliability for AWS resources through physical isolation and redundant infrastructure.
    C. AWS Availability Zones reduce the reliability of AWS resources by spreading them across multiple locations.
    D. AWS Availability Zones do not affect the reliability of AWS resources.

20. Which of the following statements best describes Amazon S3?
    A. A block storage service built to provide high-performance, block-level storage to EC2 instances
    B. A file storage service built to provide scalable storage for high-performance compute workloads
    C. An object storage service built to store and retrieve any amount of data from anywhere
    D. A file storage service built to share file systems with AWS and on-prem compute resources

21. A company is planning to deploy a new web application in the AWS Cloud using Amazon EC2. The application requires high levels of CPU and memory resources. Which of the following instance types would be the best fit for this use case?
    A. Compute optimized
    B. General purpose
    C. Memory optimized
    D. Storage optimized

22. A company is storing critical data on Amazon S3 and wants to ensure that they can recover data in case of accidental deletion or corruption. Which feature of Amazon S3 can help with this requirement?
    A. S3 Transfer Acceleration
    B. S3 Replication
    C. S3 Lifecycle Policies
    D. S3 Versioning

23. Which AWS service provides block-level storage volumes for use with Amazon EC2 instances?
    A. Amazon EBS
    B. Amazon EFS
    C. Amazon S3
    D. Amazon RDS

24. A customer needs to store data for long-term archival purposes and the data is unlikely to be accessed frequently. Which Amazon S3 storage class is the most appropriate for this use case?
    A. S3 Standard
    B. S3 Intelligent-Tiering
    C. S3 One Zone-Infrequent Access
    D. S3 Glacier

25. Which of the following statements best describes Amazon VPC?
    A. It is a fully-managed service that provides a scalable and highly available compute platform for hosting websites and applications.
    B. It is a content delivery network service that delivers static and dynamic web content to users around the world.
    C. It is a service that enables customers to run their own custom applications on AWS using a pre-built environment with all the necessary components pre-installed.
    D. It is a service that enables customers to create virtual data centers and manage their own isolated network environment in the AWS Cloud.

26. Which of the following statements about Amazon RDS Multi-AZ deployments is true?
    A. Multi-AZ deployments allow for database replication across different Regions for disaster recovery purposes.
    B. Multi-AZ deployments provide automatic scaling of compute and memory resources based on database workload.
    C. Multi-AZ deployments are only available for certain database engines, such as Amazon Aurora.
    D. Multi-AZ deployments provide high availability and automatic failover capability within the same Region.

27. Which AWS service is best suited for delivering media content, such as streaming video or audio, to users with low latency and high availability?
    A. Amazon S3

B. Amazon CloudFront

C. Amazon Elastic Transcoder

D. Amazon Kinesis Video Streams

28. A small startup is using AWS for their application and they require 24/7 support with 1-hour response time for critical issues. They do not need any personalized technical guidance or a dedicated Technical Account Manager (TAM). Which AWS Support plan should the startup choose?

    A. Basic Support
    B. Developer Support
    C. Business Support
    D. Enterprise Support

29. What is AWS Trusted Advisor and how can it help improve a customer's AWS environment?

    A. AWS Trusted Advisor is a tool that scans a customer's AWS environment and provides recommendations to optimize performance, security, and cost-efficiency.
    B. AWS Trusted Advisor is a tool that monitors a customer's AWS environment for security vulnerabilities and provides real-time alerts to help prevent security breaches.
    C. AWS Trusted Advisor is a tool that provides 24/7 technical support and personalized guidance for AWS customers.
    D. AWS Trusted Advisor is a tool that helps migrate a customer's on-premises workloads to AWS.

30. What is the customer responsible for securing in the context of EC2 instances? (Select two)

    A. The security of the underlying hardware
    B. The encryption of data stored on the instance
    C. The security of the hypervisor
    D. Patching and maintaining the operating system

31. What is AWS responsible for securing in the context of database services?
    A. The encryption of data stored in the database
    B. The security of access credentials
    C. The security of the database schema
    D. The security of the database host operating systems

32. Which AWS service can help customers monitor and protect their web applications from common web exploits, such as SQL injection and cross-site scripting attacks?
    A. AWS Shield
    B. AWS WAF
    C. Amazon Inspector
    D. Amazon GuardDuty

33. Which of the following statements best describes AWS Shield?
    A. AWS Shield is a managed service that enables logging, monitoring, and event auditing for AWS customers.
    B. AWS Shield is a managed service that provides network security and intrusion detection for AWS customers.
    C. AWS Shield is a security service that automatically detects and mitigates DDoS attacks on AWS infrastructure.
    D. AWS Shield is a security service that prevents malicious activity and detects zero-day attacks on AWS infrastructure.

34. Which of the following AWS services is primarily used for monitoring, logging, and alerting on AWS resources and applications?
    A. AWS Shield
    B. Amazon GuardDuty
    C. AWS CloudTrail
    D. Amazon CloudWatch

35. What is the maximum number of security groups that can be associated with a single network interface in Amazon VPC?
    A. 1
    B. 2
    C. 5
    D. 10

36. Which of the following is a true statement regarding VPC Flow Logs in AWS?
    A. VPC Flow Logs capture only incoming traffic to the VPC.
    B. VPC Flow Logs capture all network traffic within the VPC, including traffic between instances and to external networks.
    C. VPC Flow Logs capture only traffic to and from internet gateways.
    D. VPC Flow Logs capture only traffic within a single subnet.

37. Which AWS service enables customers to create and manage users and groups to control access to AWS resources?
    A. AWS IAM
    B. Amazon Cognito
    C. Amazon Route 53
    D. Amazon VPC

38. Which of the following is a security best practice for the AWS account root user?
    A. The root user should be used for everyday tasks to ensure consistent access.
    B. The root user's password should be the same as other user accounts to simplify management.
    C. The root user should use multi-factor authentication (MFA) to prevent unauthorized access.
    D. The root user should be deleted to ensure nobody has access to all AWS resources in the account.

39. Which AWS IAM feature can be used to assign permissions to multiple IAM users at once?
    A. IAM users

B. IAM roles
C. IAM policies
D. IAM groups

40. Which of the following is a true statement regarding AWS IAM roles?
    A. IAM roles are permanent and cannot be deleted.
    B. IAM roles can only be assumed by AWS service accounts.
    C. IAM roles should always be used to grant temporary access to AWS resources.
    D. IAM roles can only be attached to IAM users.

41. A customer wants to ensure they have access to the AMS security team for guidance on AWS security best practices and mechanisms for preventative and detective controls. What is the minimum support plan they need?
    A. Business Support
    B. Developer Support
    C. Enterprise Support
    D. Basic Support

42. Which AWS resource offers a range of security products from third-party vendors, including firewalls, intrusion detection and prevention systems, and vulnerability scanning tools?
    A. AWS Partner Network
    B. AWS Marketplace
    C. AWS Professional Services
    D. AWS Managed Services

43. A startup company is launching a new mobile application and is expecting a surge in traffic in the coming weeks due to a marketing campaign. The company is unsure about the exact number of instances needed to handle the traffic, and the workload may fluctuate frequently. Which EC2 pricing model would be the most suitable and cost-effective for this workload?
    A. Spot Instances

B. Reserved Instances
C. On-Demand Instances
D. Dedicated Instances

44. Which of the following are the primary factors that impact customer billing for Amazon S3?
    A. Amount of data stored, data transfer out, and storage class.
    B. Data transfer in, amount of data stored, and data transfer out.
    C. Storage class, number of buckets, and data transfer in.
    D. Object size, number of requests, and storage class.

45. Which EC2 pricing models ensure customers have physical hardware that is reserved for their EC2 instances? (Select two)
    A. Dedicated Instances
    B. Reserved Instances
    C. Capacity Reservations
    D. Dedicated Hosts

46. A customer wants to take advantage of volume discounts for AWS resource usage. Which AWS Organizations feature will enable this?
    A. Cost allocation tags
    B. Compliance validation
    C. Consolidated billing
    D. Service control policies

47. Which of the following statements most accurately describes AWS Organizations?
    A. AWS Organizations is a service that provides customers with interactive visualizations of their AWS usage and cost data.
    B. AWS Organizations is a service that enables customers to set custom cost and usage budgets for their AWS resources.
    C. AWS Organizations is a service that provides customers with a range of pre-built reports that provide detailed information on AWS usage and costs.

D. AWS Organizations is a service that enables customers to consolidate multiple AWS accounts under a single master account.

48. A customer wants to generate detailed information to show billing and resource usage data for specific services, time periods, and other criteria. Which AWS Billing and Cost Management feature will enable this?
    A. AWS Budgets
    B. Consolidated billing
    C. AWS Explorer
    D. AWS Cost and Usage Reports

49. Which of the following AWS services and features allows users to set custom cost and usage thresholds, and receive alerts when costs exceed the defined limits?
    A. AWS Cost Explorer
    B. AWS Budgets
    C. AWS CloudTrail
    D. AWS Config

50. How can the AWS Pricing Calculator help customers estimate their AWS costs?
    A. By providing real-time cost tracking and monitoring of their AWS resources.
    B. By providing a detailed breakdown of their monthly AWS bill.
    C. By automatically optimizing their AWS resource usage to reduce costs.
    D. By allowing them to estimate the cost of AWS services and resources before deploying them.

AWS CLF-C01 Practice Test Answer Key

The answer key shows which domain and capability each question will prepare you for. This grouping will enable you to visualize which domains you need to focus more effort on to prepare for the actual exam.

To score your practice test, give yourself 20 points for each correct answer. For questions where you selected two options, only give yourself 20 points if you selected both options correctly. When you've finished checking your answers, add up your total points. If you scored 720 points or greater out of a possible 1000 points, you have passed the test. AWS does not publish the actual scoring system they use to determine an exam taker's results. However, they do publish a passing score for the exam of 720 points out of a possible 1000. The scoring system on this practice test may not exactly match the AWS exam scoring system. However, your practice test score will give you an accurate idea of how prepared you are to pass the AWS Certified Cloud Practitioner CLF-C01 exam.

For more practice tests, visit our website at informedreadiness.com, or purchase the practice tests eBook from the author on Amazon, Apple Books, Barnes & Noble, or any store where you purchase your eBooks.

Exam Domain: Cloud Concepts

Cloud Concepts Capability: Define the AWS Cloud and its value proposition

1. Which of the following cloud computing models provides customers with the most control over the compute, storage, and networking resources delivered by a cloud provider?
   A. Application-as-a-Service (AaaS)
   B. Infrastructure-as-a-Service (IaaS)
   C. Platform-as-a-Service (PaaS)
   D. Software-as-a-Service (SaaS)

Answer: B. Infrastructure-as-a-Service (IaaS)

Infrastructure as a Service (IaaS) is a cloud computing model that delivers virtual IT infrastructure like compute, storage, and network resources on a pay-as-you-go basis over the internet. You can use IaaS to request and configure the resources you require to run your applications and IT systems. With IaaS, you are responsible for deploying, maintaining, and supporting your applications and data, as well as patching and updating any operating systems running on your cloud resources. The cloud provider is responsible for maintaining the physical infrastructure and any virtualization software required to deliver cloud resources over the network. Infrastructure-as-a-Service gives you flexibility and control over your IT resources in a cost-effective manner.

2. Which of the following statements best describes the deployment models offered by AWS?
   A. The On-premises (private cloud) deployment model allows customers to access AWS resources over the internet.
   B. The Cloud (public cloud) deployment model allows customers to access AWS resources over the internet.
   C. The Hybrid cloud deployment model allows customers to access AWS resources solely over the internet.

D. The Cloud (public Cloud) deployment model allows customers to build a cloud environment within their own data centers.

Answer: B. The Cloud (public cloud) deployment model allows customers to access AWS resources over the internet.

AWS supports public cloud (referred to as the Cloud deployment model by AWS) and hybrid cloud deployment models. Public cloud refers to services provided over the internet that can be accessed by anyone with an internet connection. Private cloud (called the on-premises deployment model by AWS) allows customers to build a cloud environment within their own data centers. Hybrid cloud refers to a combination of public and private cloud services that are integrated and managed as a single environment. AWS offers many public cloud services to customers, including Amazon EC2, EBS, and S3. AWS also offers hybrid cloud services that enable businesses to run applications in a combination of on-premises data centers and the AWS Cloud, including AWS Outposts, Storage Gateway, and Direct Connect.

3. Which AWS service can help achieve fault tolerance for applications by automatically distributing incoming traffic across multiple instances?
   A. Amazon Simple Notification Service (SNS)
   B. Amazon Elastic Compute Cloud (EC2)
   C. Amazon Elastic Load Balancing (ELB)
   D. AWS Auto Scaling

Answer: C. Amazon Elastic Load Balancing (ELB)

Amazon Elastic Load Balancing is a service that automatically distributes incoming application traffic across multiple instances or containers to improve availability and fault tolerance. With ELB, incoming traffic is automatically routed to healthy instances or containers, while unhealthy instances or containers are automatically removed from the load-balancing rotation.

4. Which of the following statements best describes the concept of elasticity in AWS?
   A. Elasticity refers to the ability of an AWS service to scale up or down automatically in response to changes in demand or traffic.
   B. Elasticity refers to the ability of an AWS service to provide unlimited resources to users, regardless of their usage patterns.
   C. Elasticity refers to the ability of an AWS service to provide high availability and fault tolerance through the use of multiple redundant resources.
   D. Elasticity refers to the ability of an AWS service to provide low latency and high throughput to users, regardless of their location.

Answer: A. Elasticity refers to the ability of an AWS service to scale up or down automatically in response to changes in demand or traffic.

AWS services like S3, RDS, and DynamoDB are designed to be elastic, meaning they can automatically adjust their capacity to match changes in demand. Other services like AWS Auto Scaling are specifically designed to automatically adjust capacity of AWS resources as demand and traffic patterns change. The built-in elasticity of AWS resources and tools like Auto Scaling enable AWS customers to optimize resource usage and minimize cost while ensuring their workloads and applications can handle sudden increases in traffic.

Cloud Concepts Capability: Identify aspects of AWS Cloud economics

5. Which AWS service enables customers to trade fixed expense for variable expense by paying only for the compute resources they use instead of making upfront capital investments in hardware and infrastructure?
   A. Amazon S3
   B. Amazon EC2
   C. AWS Elastic Beanstalk
   D. Amazon Glacier

Answer: B. Amazon EC2

Amazon EC2 (Elastic Compute Cloud) is an AWS service that provides resizable compute capacity in the cloud. With Amazon EC2, customers can quickly and easily scale their computing capacity up or down based on demand and only pay for the capacity they use. This enables customers to trade fixed expense for variable expense, and avoid the need to make upfront capital investments in hardware and infrastructure.

6. Which of the following statements is true about AWS tiered pricing?
   A. AWS tiered pricing provides a fixed cost per hour for using AWS services, regardless of the usage level.
   B. AWS tiered pricing provides a volume-based pricing model, where customers pay a fixed cost per unit of usage.
   C. AWS tiered pricing provides a customized pricing model, where customers can negotiate their own rates with AWS.
   D. AWS tiered pricing provides discounts based on the amount of usage, with lower rates for higher usage.

Answer: D. AWS tiered pricing provides discounts based on the amount of usage, with lower rates for higher usage.

AWS tiered pricing, also referred to as volume discounts, is a pricing model that provides discounts based on the amount of usage. With tiered pricing, the cost per unit of usage decreases as the usage level increases. This model is designed to be cost-effective for customers who use a large amount of AWS services and to encourage customers to use more resources as their needs grow.

7. Which of the following statements best describes how AWS fully managed services help customers save on costs?
   A. AWS fully managed services offer upfront pricing, allowing customers to easily budget for their infrastructure costs.
   B. AWS manages all underlying operating systems and software ensuring operations personnel are not required to patch and maintain systems.

C. Customers manage and maintain the underlying infrastructure and software ensuring they can configure software to their exact specifications.

D. AWS fully managed services offer more complex solutions resulting in greater return on investment.

Answer: B. AWS manages all underlying operating systems and software ensuring operations personnel are not required to patch and maintain systems.

AWS Fully Managed Services are cloud services that are fully managed and operated by AWS. This means that AWS is responsible for all aspects of the service, including the underlying infrastructure, software updates, security, and maintenance. This eliminates the need for customers to manage and maintain the infrastructure, allowing them to focus on their core business. By managing the software updates and maintenance of fully managed services, AWS ensures customers can avoid high costs associated with hiring specialized personnel to operate and maintain operating systems and other software.

8. Which AWS service helps customers stop guessing capacity and provision the exact amount of resources needed to support their applications?
   A. Amazon CloudFront
   B. Amazon Elastic Compute Cloud (EC2)
   C. AWS Auto Scaling
   D. AWS Lambda

Answer: C. AWS Auto Scaling

AWS Auto Scaling allows customers to automatically adjust their compute capacity based on demand. This eliminates the need for manual intervention and guessing how much capacity is needed. With AWS Auto Scaling, customers can set policies to automatically scale their resources up or down based on specific conditions, such as CPU utilization or network traffic. This results in cost savings and improved application performance.

Cloud Concepts Capability: Explain the different cloud architecture design principles

9. Which of the following statements best describes the AWS Well-Architected Framework?
   A. It is a set of guidelines for building secure, high-performance, resilient, cost optimized, and sustainable infrastructure in the AWS Cloud.
   B. It is a collection of pre-built architectures that can be deployed in the AWS Cloud to speed up the development process.
   C. It is a tool that helps you monitor and optimize the cost of your AWS infrastructure.
   D. It is a certification program that validates your expertise in designing and deploying applications on the AWS platform.

Answer: A. It is a set of guidelines for building secure, high-performance, resilient, cost optimized, and sustainable infrastructure in the AWS Cloud.

The AWS Well-Architected Framework provides a structured approach to help you evaluate your architectures and make informed decisions about the trade-offs between different design choices. The framework covers six pillars: operational excellence, security, reliability, performance efficiency, cost optimization, and sustainability. By following the Well-Architected Framework, you can ensure that your AWS infrastructure is designed to meet your business needs and scale to support your growth.

10. A customer wants to decouple components of a workload in the AWS Cloud. Which AWS services will enable this? (Select two)
    A. Amazon RDS
    B. Amazon API Gateway
    C. Amazon SQS
    D. Amazon S3

Answer: B and C. Amazon API Gateway and Amazon SQS

When designing workloads in the AWS Cloud, it is often a best practice to decouple components to increase reliability and scalability. One way to achieve this is by using a message queuing service to send messages between components. The Amazon Simple Queue Service (SQS) is a fully managed message queuing service that enables decoupling and scalability of microservices, distributed systems, and serverless applications. It can be used to transmit any volume of data, at any level of throughput, without losing messages or requiring other services to be available. Another way to achieve this is by using a service that provides a secure and scalable API endpoint for applications. Amazon API Gateway is a fully managed service that makes it easy for customers to create, publish, maintain, monitor, and secure APIs at any scale. By using Amazon API Gateway, customers can decouple their workload components and expose their functionality as APIs that can be accessed securely over the internet or private networks.

11. Which pillar of the AWS Well-Architected Framework focuses on ensuring that workloads are run efficiently and that organizations can continuously improve their processes and procedures?
   A. Operational Excellence
   B. Performance Efficiency
   C. Reliability
   D. Security

Answer: A. Operational Excellence

The Operational Excellence pillar of the AWS Well-Architected Framework focuses on ensuring that workloads are running efficiently and effectively, while also delivering business value. This pillar includes best practices for managing and automating infrastructure, monitoring and measuring performance, and continuously improving processes. It also emphasizes the importance of having a culture of experimentation and innovation, where teams are encouraged to test new ideas and learn from their failures. Overall, the Operational Excellence pillar aims to help customers achieve operational excellence in the AWS Cloud by enabling them to optimize their resources, reduce waste, and deliver value to their customers.

12. Which of the following statements best describes the Reliability pillar of the AWS Well-Architected Framework?
    A. It is a set of principles for achieving highly available and fault-tolerant architectures that can recover from failures in the AWS Cloud.
    B. It is a set of practices for running and monitoring your systems to deliver business value and continuously improve your processes in the AWS Cloud.
    C. It is a set of best practices for designing and operating secure and compliant IT systems in the AWS Cloud.
    D. It is a set of guidelines for designing and operating sustainable and efficient IT systems that minimize the environmental impact of your workloads.

Answer: A. It is a set of principles for achieving highly available and fault-tolerant architectures that can recover from failures in the AWS Cloud.

The Reliability pillar of the AWS Well-Architected Framework focuses on designing architectures that can recover from failures and operate continuously without interruptions. It includes best practices for designing fault-tolerant systems, implementing backup and disaster recovery procedures, and testing your systems regularly to ensure that they are reliable and fault-tolerant. This pillar also emphasizes the importance of using automation and monitoring tools to detect and respond to failures quickly and efficiently. By following the Reliability pillar, you can ensure that your systems are designed to deliver consistent and predictable performance, even in the face of unexpected events or disruptions.

13. A customer wants to think parallel in the AWS Cloud by providing shared access to a file system and improving performance. Which AWS service will enable this?
    A. Amazon S3
    B. Amazon EBS
    C. Amazon RDS
    D. Amazon EFS

Answer: D. Amazon EFS

Amazon EFS is a scalable, fully managed file storage service in the AWS Cloud that provides shared access to a common file system across multiple Amazon EC2 instances. By using Amazon EFS, customers can think parallel and improve the performance of their workloads by allowing multiple instances to read and write to the same file system concurrently. Amazon EFS is designed to provide low latency, high throughput access to files, which makes it ideal for workloads that require high levels of parallelism, such as big data analytics, media processing, and content management. With Amazon EFS, customers can easily scale their file storage capacity up or down as their workloads change, and pay only for the storage and throughput they use.

Exam Domain: Technology

Technology Capability: Define methods of deploying and operating in the AWS Cloud

14. Which of the following AWS management tools includes a set of programming libraries in various programming languages used to interact with AWS services?
    A. AWS SDKs
    B. AWS Management Console
    C. AWS CLIs
    D. Amazon API Gateway

Answer: A. AWS SDKs

The AWS SDKs (Software Development Kits) are a set of libraries and tools provided by Amazon Web Services (AWS) to help developers build applications that integrate with AWS services. The SDKs provide a convenient way for developers to interact with AWS services using their preferred programming language and development environment. AWS SDKs are available for a variety of programming languages, including Java, .NET, Python, PHP, Ruby, Go, JavaScript, and others. Each SDK includes libraries, code samples, documentation, and tools to help developers get started quickly and easily.

15. Which of the following statements are true regarding AWS Transit Gateway? (Select two)
    A. AWS Transit Gateway enables customers to connect their Amazon VPCs and on-premises networks through a single gateway.
    B. AWS Transit Gateway is limited to connecting a maximum of two VPCs.
    C. AWS Transit Gateway can only be used to connect VPCs in the AWS Cloud.
    D. AWS Transit Gateway supports both IPv4 and IPv6 traffic.

Answer: A and D. AWS Transit Gateway enables customers to connect their Amazon VPCs and on-premises networks through a single gateway and AWS Transit Gateway supports both IPv4 and IPv6 traffic.

AWS Transit Gateway is a fully managed service that simplifies the management and scaling of VPC (Virtual Private Cloud) networks. It enables customers to connect thousands of VPCs, data centers, and remote offices through a single gateway. AWS Transit Gateway acts as a hub and enables customers to establish and manage VPC and VPN (Virtual Private Network) connections in a centralized and scalable way. With AWS Transit Gateway, customer can create a single gateway that can be used to interconnect all of their VPCs and other networks, which eliminates the need for multiple VPN connections and VPC peering.

16. Which AWS service can customers use to implement hybrid cloud in the AWS Cloud and bypass the public internet to establish a private connection to AWS?
    A. Amazon Redshift
    B. Amazon VPN
    C. AWS Direct Connect
    D. Amazon CloudFront

Answer: C. AWS Direct Connect

AWS Direct Connect is a service that customers can use to establish a dedicated network connection between their on-premises infrastructure and the AWS Cloud. With AWS Direct Connect, customers can bypass the public internet and establish a private, dedicated network connection to AWS, which can improve security, increase reliability, and reduce latency. AWS Direct Connect can be used to establish a hybrid cloud environment, where some resources are located on-premises and some are located in the AWS Cloud. AWS Direct Connect can also be used to transfer large amounts of data for various use cases, such as workload migration, backups, and disaster recovery.

17. A customer wants to implement Kubernetes to run containerized applications in the AWS Cloud? Which AWS service will enable this?
    A. Amazon S3
    B. Amazon EC2
    C. Amazon ECS
    D. Amazon EKS

Answer: D. Amazon EKS

Amazon Elastic Kubernetes Service (Amazon EKS) is a fully-managed service that customers can use to run, manage, and scale Kubernetes clusters in the AWS Cloud. With Amazon EKS, customers can deploy their containers using Kubernetes without worrying about the underlying infrastructure. Amazon EKS integrates with other AWS services, such as Amazon ECR for container image registry, to enable easy and secure container deployment and management.

Technology Capability: Define the AWS global infrastructure

18. Which of the following statements best describes the purpose of AWS Regions?
    A. AWS Regions provide low-latency connectivity between AWS services.
    B. AWS Regions are used to manage access control and security for AWS resources.
    C. AWS Regions are used to specify the geographic location of AWS resources.
    D. AWS Regions are used to reduce the cost of running AWS resources.

Answer: C. AWS Regions are used to specify the geographic location of AWS resources.

AWS Regions are separate geographic locations around the world where AWS has data centers. Each Region is made up of multiple Availability Zones, which are isolated data centers within a Region that are connected with low latency, high-throughput networks. AWS customers can choose the Region where they want to host their applications and data based on factors such as latency, compliance, and data sovereignty requirements. By choosing a Region close to their users, customers can reduce the latency and improve the performance of their applications.

19. Which of the following statements best describes the relationship between AWS Availability Zones and reliability?
    A. AWS Availability Zones are the only way to achieve high reliability for AWS resources.
    B. AWS Availability Zones provide an additional layer of reliability for AWS resources through physical isolation and redundant infrastructure.
    C. AWS Availability Zones reduce the reliability of AWS resources by spreading them across multiple locations.
    D. AWS Availability Zones do not affect the reliability of AWS resources.

Answer: B. AWS Availability Zones provide an additional layer of reliability for AWS resources through physical isolation and redundant infrastructure.

AWS Availability Zones (AZs) are isolated data centers within a Region that are interconnected through high-speed, low-latency links. Each AZ is designed to be independent of other AZs within the same Region, which provides fault tolerance, high availability, and scalability for AWS customers. Each AZ is designed with its own redundant power, cooling, and networking improving reliability of the infrastructure hosting AWS services and customer applications. AWS customers can deploy their applications and services across multiple AZs within a Region to achieve high availability and fault tolerance.

Technology Capability: Identify the core AWS services

20. Which of the following statements best describes Amazon S3?
    A. A block storage service built to provide high-performance, block-level storage to EC2 instances
    B. A file storage service built to provide scalable storage for high-performance compute workloads
    C. An object storage service built to store and retrieve any amount of data from anywhere
    D. A file storage service built to share file systems with AWS and on-prem compute resources

Answer: C. An object storage service built to store and retrieve any amount of data from anywhere

Amazon Simple Storage Service (S3) is an object storage service offering industry-leading scalability, data availability, security, and performance. AWS customers of all sizes and industries can store and protect any amount of data with S3 for virtually any use case, such as data lakes, cloud-native applications, and mobile apps. With cost-effective storage classes and easy-to-use management features, Amazon S3 enables customers to optimize costs, organize data, and configure fine-tuned access controls to meet specific business, organizational, and compliance requirements.

21. A company is planning to deploy a new web application in the AWS Cloud using Amazon EC2. The application requires high levels of CPU and memory resources. Which of the following instance types would be the best fit for this use case?
    A. Compute optimized
    B. General purpose
    C. Memory optimized
    D. Storage optimized

Answer: B. General purpose

For a web application that requires high levels of CPU and memory resources, the general purpose instance type would be the best fit. The EC2 general purpose instance type is optimized for workloads that require a balance of compute, memory, storage, and network resources. EC2 general purpose instances are versatile, cost-effective instances designed to handle a wide range of workloads, including web applications, small and medium databases, and development and testing environments.

22. A company is storing critical data on Amazon S3 and wants to ensure that they can recover data in case of accidental deletion or corruption. Which feature of Amazon S3 can help with this requirement?
    A. S3 Transfer Acceleration
    B. S3 Replication
    C. S3 Lifecycle Policies
    D. S3 Versioning

Answer: D. S3 Versioning

S3 Versioning is a feature of Amazon S3 that enables customers to store multiple versions of an object in the same bucket. This feature helps customers protect against accidental deletion, overwrite, and corruption of data. With S3 Versioning, a customer can easily recover a previous version of an object if necessary.

23. Which AWS service provides block-level storage volumes for use with Amazon EC2 instances?
    A. Amazon EBS
    B. Amazon EFS
    C. Amazon S3
    D. Amazon RDS

Answer: A. Amazon EBS

Amazon Elastic Block Store (EBS) provides block-level storage volumes for use with Amazon EC2 instances. EBS volumes are highly available and reliable storage volumes that can be attached to any running instance that is in the same Availability Zone as the volume. They are designed for use with applications that require persistent storage, such as databases, file systems, and applications that require access to raw block-level storage.

24. A customer needs to store data for long-term archival purposes and the data is unlikely to be accessed frequently. Which Amazon S3 storage class is the most appropriate for this use case?
    A. S3 Standard
    B. S3 Intelligent-Tiering
    C. S3 One Zone-Infrequent Access
    D. S3 Glacier

Answer: D. S3 Glacier

S3 Glacier is an Amazon S3 storage class that is designed for long-term backup and archive storage of data that is rarely accessed but needs to be retained for compliance or regulatory reasons. It offers retrieval times ranging from minutes to hours and is the most cost-effective storage class for long-term data archival.

25. Which of the following statements best describes Amazon VPC?
    A. It is a fully-managed service that provides a scalable and highly available compute platform for hosting websites and applications.
    B. It is a content delivery network service that delivers static and dynamic web content to users around the world.
    C. It is a service that enables customers to run their own custom applications on AWS using a pre-built environment with all the necessary components pre-installed.
    D. It is a service that enables customers to create virtual data centers and manage their own isolated network environment in the AWS Cloud.

Answer: D. It is a service that enables customers to create virtual data centers and manage their own isolated network environment in the AWS Cloud.

Amazon VPC (Virtual Private Cloud) is a service that enables customers to create a virtual network environment in the AWS (Amazon Web Services) cloud that is logically isolated from other virtual networks and the public internet. With Amazon VPC, customers can launch Amazon EC2 instances and other AWS resources in a virtual data center that they define giving them complete control over their virtual networking environment, including selection of their IP address range, creation of subnets, and configuration of route tables and network gateways.

26. Which of the following statements about Amazon RDS Multi-AZ deployments is true?
    A. Multi-AZ deployments allow for database replication across different Regions for disaster recovery purposes.
    B. Multi-AZ deployments provide automatic scaling of compute and memory resources based on database workload.
    C. Multi-AZ deployments are only available for certain database engines, such as Amazon Aurora.
    D. Multi-AZ deployments provide high availability and automatic failover capability within the same Region.

Answer: D. Multi-AZ deployments provide high availability and automatic failover capability within the same Region.

Multi-AZ deployments are designed to increase availability and reliability of an Amazon RDS database within a single Region by replicating the primary database instance to a standby instance located in a different Availability Zone (AZ). This provides high availability and automatic failover capability in the event of a primary instance failure or maintenance event. Multi-AZ deployments are available for all RDS supported database engines, including Amazon Aurora, MySQL, PostgreSQL, Oracle, and SQL Server.

27. Which AWS service is best suited for delivering media content, such as streaming video or audio, to users with low latency and high availability?
   A. Amazon S3
   B. Amazon CloudFront
   C. Amazon Elastic Transcoder
   D. Amazon Kinesis Video Streams

Answer: B. Amazon CloudFront

Amazon CloudFront is a global content delivery network (CDN) service offered by AWS (Amazon Web Services) that enables customers to securely deliver static and dynamic web content, including streaming video and audio, to users worldwide with low latency and high data transfer speeds.

Technology Capability: Identify resources for technology support

28. A small startup is using AWS for their application and they require 24/7 support with 1-hour response time for critical issues. They do not need any personalized technical guidance or a dedicated Technical Account Manager (TAM). Which AWS Support plan should the startup choose?
   A. Basic Support
   B. Developer Support
   C. Business Support
   D. Enterprise Support

Answer: C. Business Support

Business Support provides 24/7 technical support and guaranteed response times of 1 hour for critical issues. While it doesn't include a dedicated TAM, it provides access to AWS Trusted Advisor, which can help the startup optimize their infrastructure for performance, security, and cost savings. The Basic Support plan only provides access to AWS Trusted Advisor checks and documentation, without any technical support. The Developer Support plan provides technical support during business hours with no guaranteed response times. The Enterprise Support plan provides a dedicated TAM and Infrastructure Event Management, which may not be necessary for the startup's needs, and it comes at a higher cost. Therefore, the best option for the startup is AWS Business Support.

29. What is AWS Trusted Advisor and how can it help improve a customer's AWS environment?
    A. AWS Trusted Advisor is a tool that scans a customer's AWS environment and provides recommendations to optimize performance, security, and cost-efficiency.
    B. AWS Trusted Advisor is a tool that monitors a customer's AWS environment for security vulnerabilities and provides real-time alerts to help prevent security breaches.
    C. AWS Trusted Advisor is a tool that provides 24/7 technical support and personalized guidance for AWS customers.
    D. AWS Trusted Advisor is a tool that helps migrate a customer's on-premises workloads to AWS.

Answer: A. AWS Trusted Advisor is a tool that scans a customer's AWS environment and provides recommendations to optimize performance, security, and cost-efficiency.

AWS Trusted Advisor is a tool that analyzes a customer's AWS environment and provides recommendations in four categories: cost optimization, performance, security, and fault tolerance. Trusted Advisor provides best practice recommendations in these categories based on AWS architecture and operational expertise. These recommendations can help improve a customer's AWS environment by reducing costs, improving performance and security, and increasing fault tolerance.

Exam Domain: Security & Compliance

Security & Compliance Capability: Define the AWS shared responsibility model

30. What is the customer responsible for securing in the context of EC2 instances? (Select two)
    A. The security of the underlying hardware
    B. The encryption of data stored on the instance
    C. The security of the hypervisor
    D. Patching and maintaining the operating system

Answer: B and D. The encryption of data stored on the instance and patching and maintaining the operating system

In the shared responsibility model, the customer is responsible for securing their applications, data, and access management, while AWS is responsible for the security of the underlying infrastructure. For EC2 instances, the customer is responsible for securing the data stored on the instance. This includes encrypting sensitive data at rest and in transit, and configuring appropriate access controls to limit access to the data. The customer is also responsible for securing the applications running on the instance by implementing appropriate security measures such as firewalls, intrusion detection and prevention systems, and anti-virus software. The customer is also responsible for patching and maintaining the operating system used by their EC2 instances. This includes keeping the operating system up to date with the latest security patches and updates to address any known vulnerabilities or exploits. Failure to patch and maintain the operating system can leave the instance and the customer's data vulnerable to cyber attacks and other security threats. AWS is responsible for the security of the data centers, the underlying hardware, and the virtualization layer. AWS provides various security tools and services that the customer can use to enhance the security of their EC2 instances, such as AWS Config, AWS CloudTrail, and AWS Security Hub.

31. What is AWS responsible for securing in the context of database services?
    A. The encryption of data stored in the database
    B. The security of access credentials
    C. The security of the database schema
    D. The security of the database host operating system

Answer: D. The security of the database host operating system

AWS provides a range of managed database services such as Amazon RDS, Amazon DynamoDB, and Amazon Aurora. In the shared responsibility model, AWS is responsible for securing the underlying infrastructure for fully managed services, including the security of the database servers and the operating systems installed on them. The security responsibility of AWS includes access controls to the data center, power and cooling systems, and the physical hardware. AWS also takes care of backups, replication, and high availability of the database instances. However, the customer is responsible for securing their data, access credentials, and database schema. This includes configuring proper database access controls, encrypting sensitive data at rest and in transit, and implementing appropriate security measures for protecting their databases against attacks and unauthorized access.

Security & Compliance Capability: Define AWS Cloud security and compliance concepts

32. Which AWS service can help customers monitor and protect their web applications from common web exploits, such as SQL injection and cross-site scripting attacks?
    A. AWS Shield
    B. AWS WAF
    C. Amazon Inspector
    D. Amazon GuardDuty

Answer: B. AWS WAF

AWS WAF (Web Application Firewall) is a service that helps customers protect their web applications from common web exploits by allowing them to create custom security rules that block common attack patterns like SQL injection and cross-site scripting. WAF also integrates with other AWS services like Amazon CloudFront, Amazon API Gateway, and Application Load Balancer to provide comprehensive protection against web attacks.

33. Which of the following statements best describes AWS Shield?
    A. AWS Shield is a managed service that enables logging, monitoring, and event auditing for AWS customers.
    B. AWS Shield is a managed service that provides network security and intrusion detection for AWS customers.
    C. AWS Shield is a security service that automatically detects and mitigates DDoS attacks on AWS infrastructure.
    D. AWS Shield is a security service that prevents malicious activity and detects zero-day attacks on AWS infrastructure.

Answer: C. AWS Shield is a security service that automatically detects and mitigates DDoS attacks on AWS infrastructure.

AWS Shield is a managed service that provides automatic DDoS protection to all AWS customers. It is designed to detect and mitigate DDoS attacks on AWS infrastructure, such as Elastic Load Balancing, Amazon CloudFront, and Amazon Route 53. AWS Shield is available in both standard and advanced versions. The standard version is available to all AWS customers at no additional cost and provides automated protections against common, most frequently occurring DDoS attacks. The advanced version provides additional protections and is recommended for customers with more complex architectures or compliance requirements.

34. Which of the following AWS services is primarily used for monitoring, logging, and alerting on AWS resources and applications?
    A. AWS Shield
    B. Amazon GuardDuty

C. AWS CloudTrail
D. Amazon CloudWatch

Answer: D. Amazon CloudWatch

Amazon CloudWatch is a monitoring service offered by Amazon Web Services (AWS) that provides real-time monitoring and logging capabilities for AWS resources and applications. It allows customers to collect and track metrics, collect and monitor log files, and set alarms on certain thresholds. CloudWatch provides dashboards that allow customers to visualize and analyze their monitoring data, as well as alarms that can be set to notify them when certain metrics reach specific thresholds. These alarms can be configured to send notifications to various AWS services or even to external services such as email or SMS.

35. What is the maximum number of security groups that can be associated with a single network interface in Amazon VPC?
    A. 1
    B. 2
    C. 5
    D. 10

Answer: C. 5

In Amazon VPC, a network interface can be associated with up to 5 security groups. A security group acts as a virtual firewall that controls the inbound and outbound traffic for the associated network interface. When a network interface is launched, you can associate it with one or more security groups. You can also modify the security groups associated with an existing network interface.

36. Which of the following is a true statement regarding VPC Flow Logs in AWS?
    A. VPC Flow Logs capture only incoming traffic to the VPC.
    B. VPC Flow Logs capture all network traffic within the VPC, including traffic between instances and to external networks.

C. VPC Flow Logs capture only traffic to and from internet gateways.
D. VPC Flow Logs capture only traffic within a single subnet.

Answer: B. VPC Flow Logs capture all network traffic within the VPC, including traffic between instances and to external networks.

VPC Flow Logs is a feature provided by Amazon Web Services (AWS) that enables customers to capture information about the IP traffic flowing into and out of their Amazon Virtual Private Cloud (VPC). VPC Flow Logs captures information about each IP packet, such as source and destination IP addresses, port numbers, and protocols used, and stores this information in a log file. These logs can be used to troubleshoot connectivity issues, analyze traffic patterns, detect and investigate security incidents, and meet compliance requirements. VPC Flow Logs can be published to Amazon CloudWatch Logs, Amazon S3, or both, allowing customers to analyze their VPC traffic in real-time or at a later time.

Security & Compliance Capability: Identify AWS access management capabilities

37. Which AWS service enables customers to create and manage users and groups to control access to AWS resources?
    A. AWS IAM
    B. Amazon Cognito
    C. Amazon Route 53
    D. Amazon VPC

Answer: A. AWS IAM

AWS Identity and Access Management (IAM) is an AWS service that enables customers to manage access to their AWS resources. IAM enables customers to create and manage AWS users and groups and to assign permissions that determine which AWS resources the users and groups can access and what they can do when they access the resources. IAM also provides features for managing security credentials, such as access keys and passwords, and for enabling multi-factor authentication (MFA) to provide additional security for AWS accounts.

38. Which of the following is a security best practice for the AWS account root user?
    A. The root user should be used for everyday tasks to ensure consistent access.
    B. The root user's password should be the same as other user accounts to simplify management.
    C. The root user should use multi-factor authentication (MFA) to prevent unauthorized access.
    D. The root user should be deleted to ensure nobody has access to all AWS resources in the account.

Answer: C. The root user should use multi-factor authentication (MFA) to prevent unauthorized access.

The AWS account root user is the user automatically created when an AWS account is first created. The root user has complete access to and control over all AWS resources in the account. Therefore, it is a best practice to use it only for account-level tasks that require root user credentials such as changing account settings, closing an AWS account and registering as a seller in the Reserved Instance Marketplace. It is also a security best practice to enable multi-factor authentication (MFA) for the root user to help prevent unauthorized access to the account. Multi-factor authentication (MFA) is an additional layer of security that requires users to provide multiple forms of authentication in order to access their AWS resources or log in to their account. This helps to prevent unauthorized access to an AWS account, even if an attacker is able to obtain a user's password.

39. Which AWS IAM feature can be used to assign permissions to multiple IAM users at once?
    A. IAM users
    B. IAM roles
    C. IAM policies
    D. IAM groups

Answer: D. IAM groups

In AWS Identity and Access Management (IAM), groups are collections of IAM users. They are used to simplify the management of permissions by allowing users to be assigned a set of permissions based on their role or job function, rather than individually. For example, a customer might create a group called "Developers" and assign it a set of permissions that allow members of that group to access development resources, such as Amazon EC2 instances or Amazon S3 buckets. Users can then be added or removed from the group as needed, and their permissions will automatically be updated based on their group membership.

40. Which of the following is a true statement regarding AWS IAM roles?
    A. IAM roles are permanent and cannot be deleted.
    B. IAM roles can only be assumed by AWS service accounts.
    C. IAM roles should always be used to grant temporary access to AWS resources.
    D. IAM roles can only be attached to IAM users.

Answer: C. IAM roles should always be used to grant temporary access to AWS resources.

AWS Identity and Access Management (IAM) roles are a secure way to grant temporary permissions to entities in AWS, such as AWS services, IAM users, or applications running on Amazon EC2 instances. IAM roles eliminate the need to share long-term security credentials, such as access keys, between entities, which helps improve security posture and reduce the risk of unauthorized access. It is an AWS security best practice to use IAM roles to grant temporary access and permissions to AWS resources and application components rather than sharing security credentials.

Security & Compliance Capability: Identify resources for security support

41. A customer wants to ensure they have access to the AMS security team for guidance on AWS security best practices and mechanisms for preventative and detective controls. What is the minimum support plan they need?
    A. Business Support
    B. Developer Support
    C. Enterprise Support
    D. Basic Support

Answer: A. Business Support

The AWS Managed Services (AMS) security team is a team of experts that work closely with customers to understand their security requirements and provide guidance on best practices for securing their workload in the AWS Cloud. Customers with a Business, Enterprise, or Enterprise On-Ramp support plan have access to the AMS security team.

42. Which AWS resource offers a range of security products from third-party vendors, including firewalls, intrusion detection and prevention systems, and vulnerability scanning tools?
    A. AWS Partner Network
    B. AWS Marketplace
    C. AWS Professional Services
    D. AWS Managed Services

Answer: B. AWS Marketplace

The AWS Marketplace is an online store that allows customers to easily find, purchase, and deploy third-party software products that are optimized to run on AWS. The Marketplace offers a broad range of software products across various categories, including security, networking, storage, databases, and more. Customers can search the AWS Marketplace for software products that meet their needs and quickly launch them with just a few clicks. The Marketplace offers both free and paid products, with pricing options that range from hourly to annual subscriptions.

Exam Domain: Billing & Pricing

Billing & Pricing Capability: Compare and contrast the various pricing models for AWS

43. A startup company is launching a new mobile application and is expecting a surge in traffic in the coming weeks due to a marketing campaign. The company is unsure about the exact number of instances needed to handle the traffic, and the workload may fluctuate frequently. Which EC2 pricing model would be the most suitable and cost-effective for this workload?
    A. Spot Instances
    B. Reserved Instances
    C. On-Demand Instances
    D. Dedicated Instances

Answer: C. On-Demand Instances

Since the company is unsure about the exact number of instances needed to handle the traffic, and the workload may fluctuate frequently, it would be best to pay for the instances on an hourly basis. This provides flexibility to scale up or down as needed, without any upfront commitments or long-term contracts. On-Demand instances are best suited for workloads with unpredictable traffic or short-term workloads. The EC2 On-Demand Instance Pricing Model is a pay-as-you-go pricing model that allows users to pay for compute capacity by the hour, with no long-term commitments or upfront fees. It's ideal for applications that have short-term, unpredictable, or spiky workloads.

44. Which of the following are the primary factors that impact customer billing for Amazon S3?
    A. Amount of data stored, data transfer out, and storage class.

B. Data transfer in, amount of data stored, and data transfer out.
C. Storage class, number of buckets, and data transfer in.
D. Object size, number of requests, and storage class.

Answer: A. Amount of data stored, data transfer out, and storage class.

Amazon S3 (Simple Storage Service) is a cloud-based object storage service that offers a flexible and simple pricing model based on the amount of data stored, data transfer out, and storage class. Although customers are charged for data transferred out of Amazon S3 to the internet or other Regions, the amount of data transferred into Amazon S3 is free. The pricing for different storage classes varies and is primarily based on the frequency of access to the data and durability requirements.

45. Which EC2 pricing models ensure customers have physical hardware that is reserved for their EC2 instances? (Select two)
    A. Dedicated Instances
    B. Reserved Instances
    C. Capacity Reservations
    D. Dedicated Hosts

Answer: A and D. Dedicated Instances and Dedicated Hosts

Dedicated Instances is a pricing model for Amazon EC2 instances that enables customers to have instances running on hardware that's dedicated to them. This pricing model is best suited for customers who have compliance or regulatory requirements that require them to have instances running on hardware that does not share resources with any other customers. Dedicated Hosts is a pricing model for EC2 instances that allows customers to have physical servers dedicated to running their instances. This pricing model is best suited for customers who have regulatory or compliance requirements or licensing agreements that require them to have dedicated physical servers and control over the placement of their instances. Customers can launch instances on Dedicated Hosts just like they would any other EC2 instances, but they have visibility and control over the underlying physical server, including the placement of instances on the server. Dedicated Hosts and Dedicated Instances can be purchased on-demand, or they can be reserved for one or three-year terms for a discounted hourly rate.

Billing & Pricing Capability: Recognize the various account structures in relation to AWS billing and pricing

46. A customer wants to take advantage of volume discounts for AWS resource usage. Which AWS Organizations feature will enable this?
    A. Cost allocation tags
    B. Compliance validation
    C. Consolidated billing
    D. Service control policies

Answer: C. Consolidated billing

Consolidated billing is a feature in AWS Organizations that enables customers to consolidate payments for multiple AWS accounts under a single paying account. This feature enables customers to take advantage of volume discounts offered by AWS. AWS offers volume discounts for many of its services, which are based on the amount of usage across all accounts in an organization. When a customer enables consolidated billing, all usage across all member accounts is aggregated, which can help achieve the usage levels required for volume discounts. Consolidated billing provides several benefits in addition to enabling volume discounts. It simplifies the billing process reducing the administrative burden of managing multiple accounts. It also provides better visibility into usage and costs across the organization making it easier to track spending and identify cost-saving opportunities. Finally, it can also help customers to negotiate better pricing with AWS, since they can use their total usage across all accounts as leverage.

47. Which of the following statements most accurately describes AWS Organizations?
    A. AWS Organizations is a service that provides customers with interactive visualizations of their AWS usage and cost data.

B. AWS Organizations is a service that enables customers to set custom cost and usage budgets for their AWS resources.
C. AWS Organizations is a service that provides customers with a range of pre-built reports that provide detailed information on AWS usage and costs.
D. AWS Organizations is a service that enables customers to consolidate multiple AWS accounts under a single master account.

Answer: D. AWS Organizations is a service that enables customers to consolidate multiple AWS accounts under a single master account.

AWS Organizations is a service that enables users to consolidate multiple AWS accounts into an organization that is centrally managed and governed. It provides a unified view of all AWS accounts and allows users to automate account creation, management, and governance. Key features of AWS Organizations include consolidated billing, account management, policy-based governance, service control policies, and cross-account access.

Billing & Pricing Capability: Identify resources available for billing support

48. A customer wants to generate detailed information to show billing and resource usage data for specific services, time periods, and other criteria. Which AWS Billing and Cost Management feature will enable this?
    A. AWS Budgets
    B. Consolidated billing
    C. AWS Explorer
    D. AWS Cost and Usage Reports

Answer: D. AWS Cost and Usage Reports

AWS Cost and Usage Reports is an AWS Billing and Cost Management feature that enables customers to access and analyze detailed information about their AWS costs and usage. Customers can generate the reports to provide a granular view of the costs incurred by AWS services allowing them to analyze and optimize their usage to reduce costs. With Cost and Usage Reports, customers can break down their costs by the hour, day, or month, by product or product resource, and by resource tags that they define themselves.

49. Which of the following AWS services allows users to set custom cost and usage thresholds and receive alerts when costs exceed defined limits?
    A. AWS Cost Explorer
    B. AWS Budgets
    C. AWS CloudTrail
    D. AWS Config

Answer: B. AWS Budgets

AWS Budgets is an AWS Billing and Cost Management feature that enables customers to set custom cost and usage thresholds, or budgets, and receive alerts when costs exceed the defined limits. With AWS Budgets, users can set budgets based on various criteria, including AWS service, Region, account, and resource tag. Users can also specify the frequency and type of alerts they receive, such as email notifications or SMS messages. AWS Budgets provides a flexible and customizable way for users to manage their costs and ensure they stay within their budget.

50. How can the AWS Pricing Calculator help customers estimate their AWS costs?
    A. By providing real-time cost tracking and monitoring of their AWS resources.
    B. By providing a detailed breakdown of their monthly AWS bill.
    C. By automatically optimizing their AWS resource usage to reduce costs.
    D. By allowing them to estimate the cost of AWS services and resources before deploying them.

Answer: D. By allowing them to estimate the cost of AWS services and resources before deploying them.

The AWS Pricing Calculator is a free tool that enables customers to estimate the cost of using AWS services and resources before they deploy them. It provides a detailed breakdown of the estimated costs, including any applicable discounts, based on the usage a customer specifies. This can help AWS customers make informed decisions about which AWS services and resources to use and how to configure them to meet their specific needs while staying within their budget.

For more practice tests, visit our website at informedreadiness.com, or purchase the practice tests book from the author on Amazon, Apple Books, Barnes & Noble, or any online store where you purchase your books
.

Dear Reader,

Congratulations! You have completed the journey through this study guide. I hope that it has provided you with a clear understanding of the exam topics and confidence to ace the AWS Certified Cloud Practitioner CLF-C01 exam.

By now, you have a unique perspective on the contents of this book. Your experiences, insights, and thoughts can be incredibly valuable to others who aspire to take the same journey you have. That's why I kindly ask you to consider leaving a review for this book on the platform where you purchased it.

Share your journey, the challenges you overcame, and the impact this book had on your preparation. This way, you can help future readers gauge if this guide is right for them. Furthermore, your feedback will also provide me with valuable insights to make improvements and provide the best possible resources for learners like you.

Remember, your voice has the power to influence and inspire others in their journey to becoming an AWS Certified Cloud Practitioner.

Thank you for your time, effort, and commitment to learning. We look forward to hearing about your successes and experiences.

Good luck with your exam!

Best wishes,
Peter Pazurek

AWS Certified Cloud Practitioner CLF-C01 Exam Study Guide

Peter Pazurek

Published by Informed Readiness
https://informedreadiness.com
support@informedreadiness.com

© 2023 Informed Readiness

All rights reserved. No portion of this book may be reproduced in any form without permission from the publisher, except as permitted by U.S. copyright law.

Printed in Great Britain
by Amazon